Chances Are

Chances Are

Hands-on Activities
in Probability and Statistics,
Grades 3-7

Sheila Dolgowich

Helen M. Lounsbury

Barry G. Muldoon

TEACHER IDEAS PRESS
A Division of
Libraries Unlimited, Inc.
Englewood, Colorado
1995

TEACHER IDEAS PRESS
A Division of Libraries Unlimited, Inc.
P.O. Box 6633
Englewood, CO 80155-6633
1-800-237-6124

Project and Copy Editor: Jason Cook
Proofreader: Suzanne Hawkins Burke
Typesetting and Interior Design: Judy Gay Matthews
Illustrations: Barry G. Muldoon

Library of Congress Cataloging-in-Publication Data

Dolgowich, Sheila.
    Chances are : hands-on activities in probability and statistics,
grades 3-7 / Sheila Dolgowich, Helen M. Lounsbury, Barry G. Muldoon.
    xviii, 126 p. 22x28 cm.
    Includes bibliographical references.
    ISBN 1-56308-314-0
    1. Probabilities--Study and teaching (Elementary) 2. Mathematical
statistics--Study and teaching (Elementary)   I. Lounsbury, Helen M.
II. Muldoon, Barry G.   III. Title.
QA273.2.D65 1995
372.7--dc20   94-40524
                                                        CIP

We would like to thank the teachers and students who field-tested Chances Are. *We are also grateful to the many educators who provided us with their advice and assistance.*

Contents

Introduction xi

How to Use This Book xv

Scope and Sequence xvii

Activity 1—SAM's Crayon Craziness 3
    Teacher's Guide 3
    SAM's Crayon Craziness 5
    Answer Key 6

Activity 2—Traffic Stopper 7
    Teacher's Guide 7
    Traffic Stopper 9
    Traffic Stopper Lens Cutouts 10
    Traffic Light 11
    Answer Key 12

Activity 3—Creative Creatures 13
    Teacher's Guide 13
    Creative Creatures 15
    Creative Creatures Cutouts 16
    Answer Key 17

**Activity 4—Menu Madness (SAMburgers, Deli SAMwiches,
Ben & Cherries)** 18
    Teacher's Guide 18
    SAMburgers 21
    SAMburgers Menu 22
    SAMburgers Cutouts 23
    Answer Key—SAMburgers 25
    Deli SAMwiches 26
    Deli SAMwiches Menu 27
    Deli SAMwiches Cutouts 28
    Answer Key—Deli SAMwiches 30
    Ben & Cherries 31
    Ben & Cherries Menu 32
    Ben & Cherries Cutouts 33
    Answer Key—Ben & Cherries 35

Activity 5—It's a Wrap! 36
    Teacher's Guide 36
    It's a Wrap! 38
    Deli SAMwiches Menu 39
    Answer Key 40

Activity 6—Dressing up Probability 41
Teacher's Guide 41
Dressing up Probability 44
Dressing up Probability Cutouts 45
Dressing up Probability Chalkboard Cutouts 47
Dressing up Probability Chalkboard Cutouts 48
Probability Tree for a Three-Child Family (extension) 49
Answer Key 50

Activity 7—Painter's Cap Possibilities 51
Teacher's Guide 51
Painter's Cap Possibilities 53
Answer Key 54

Activity 8—SAM and Samantha's Family Tree 55
Teacher's Guide 55
SAM and Samantha's Family Tree 57
Answer Key 58

Activity 9—See How They Run 59
Teacher's Guide 59
See How They Run 61
See How They Run Tree Diagram 62
See How They Run Tree Diagram—Answer Key 63
See How They Run—Answer Key 64

Activity 10—Probability Spin-Off 65
Teacher's Guide 65
Probability Spin-Off 67
Spinner Construction Instructions 68
Answer Key 69

Activity 11—Qwerty Questions 70
Teacher's Guide 70
Qwerty Questions 72
Qwerty Questions Frequency Chart 73

Activity 12—Peeking at Presidents 74
Teacher's Guide 74
Peeking at Presidents 76
Presidents Chart (part a) 77
Presidents Chart (part b) 78

Activity 13—Poll Cats 79
Teacher's Guide 79
Poll Cats 81
Poll Cats Follow-up Questions 82

Assessment 83
    Pre-Program Parent Letter 85
    Pre-Program Parent Survey 86
    Pre-Program Self-Assessment 87
    Evaluating Student Behavior 89
    Group Assessment 90
    Follow-up Parent Letter 91
    Follow-up Parent Survey 92
    Follow-up Self-Assessment 93
    Chances Are Certificate of Accomplishment 95

Student Journal 96
    Cover Page 97
    SAM's Crayon Craziness—Journal Entry for Activity 1 98
    Traffic Stopper—Journal Entry for Activity 2 99
    Creative Creatures—Journal Entry for Activity 3 100
    Menu Madness—Journal Entry for Activity 4 101
    It's a Wrap!—Journal Entry for Activity 5 102
    Dressing up Probability—Journal Entry for Activity 6 103
    Painter's Cap Possibilities—Journal Entry for Activity 7 104
    SAM and Samantha's Family Tree—Journal Entry for Activity 8 105
    See How They Run—Journal Entry for Activity 9 106
    Probability Spin-Off—Journal Entry for Activity 10 107
    Qwerty Questions—Journal Entry for Activity 11 108
    Peeking at Presidents—Journal Entry for Activity 12 109
    Poll Cats—Journal Entry for Activity 13 110

Appendix 111
    Curriculum and Evaluation Standards for School Mathematics 113
    Making Manipulatives 113

Glossary 115

References 121

About the Authors 125

Introduction

Chances Are is designed to provide hands-on experiences in probability and statistics, an often overlooked topic in the elementary mathematics curriculum. Sense-Able Mathematics is a name that reflects the sensory nature of the activities in this book; it also lent itself to the development of our mascot, SAM the mouse. *Chances Are* is intended to be used by students and teachers in grades 3-7. It incorporates recent educational research on curriculum, assessment, and instruction and reflects the National Council of Teachers of Mathematics (NCTM) standards that pertain to probability and statistics (listed in the appendix).

Teaching-effectiveness researchers have found that the achievement of basic skills by elementary students is promoted by directed instruction (Brophy and Good 1986, 326-75; Rosenshine and Stevens 1984, 745-49). During directed instruction, the teachers increase the effectiveness of their teaching by

- presenting students with new information that is structured;

- assisting students in relating the new information to their prior knowledge;

- systematically monitoring students' performance and providing corrective feedback during drill, recitation, and practice activities; and

- encouraging students to maintain a high level of engagement in their academic tasks.

The directed activities and assessment tools in this book are geared to meet these criteria for effective teaching.

Based on research, Brophy and Good believe that these principles apply to "any body of knowledge or set of skills that has been sufficiently well-organized and analyzed so it can be presented (explained, modeled) systematically and then practiced or applied during activities that call for performance that can be evaluated for quality and where incorrect or imperfect given appropriate feedback" (1986, 130). Peterson and Janicki (1979); Peterson, Janicki, and Swing (1981); and Peterson, Wilkinson, Spinelli, and Swing (1984) have found that small-group cooperative learning also may be an effective adjunct to whole-class instruction in the traditional elementary mathematics classroom. Peterson, Wilkinson, Spinelli, and Swing (1984) indicate in their research that students learn by helping other students, by explaining their answers, by explaining to other students why their answers are incorrect, and by receiving explanations that describe appropriate problem-solving processes and strategies. Other researchers such as Kirby (1984), Pressley and Levin (1983a, 1983b), and Weinstein and Mayer (1986), have found that students benefit from training in the following cognitive strategies:

- memory strategies

- elaboration strategies

- comprehension monitoring

- self-questioning

- rehearsal strategies

- planning and goal setting

- comprehension strategies

- verbal self-instruction and self-regulation

- problem-solving strategies

- hypothesis generation

- study skills

For these reasons, many of the activities in this book are designed to be done by learning pairs or groups. Opportunity is provided for discussion and presentation of ideas and sharing of strategies. The student journal provides an effective method of using such strategies as hypothesis generation, self-questioning, and elaboration. The "How to Use This Book" section, following this introduction, offers more detailed suggestions for the teacher to use in implementing the activities and assessment tools provided.

To get a sense of meaning and understanding from academic mathematical tasks, Doyle concludes, activities must be unstructured enough to allow students to "discover" generalizations and invent algorithms (rules or methods for solving a particular type of problem) on their own (1983).

Bruner believes that "an understanding of fundamental principles and ideas . . . appears to be the main road to adequate 'transfer of training'" and that the learning of "general or fundamental principles" ensures that individuals can reconstruct details when memory fails (1960, 25). *Chances Are* provides an introduction to the fundamental principles and ideas of probability and statistics and allows students to explore and "discover" many of the basic algorithms on their own.

Bruner's work (1960) is grounded in Piaget's stage-theory. Bruner identifies three levels of representation that he considers essential to the learning of a child: the enactive level (direct manipulation of objects), the iconic level (manipulation of mental images of objects), and the symbolic level (manipulation of symbols). With this in mind, we recommend a "spiral curriculum," a curriculum in which the same ideas are repeated and expanded into increasingly complex, increasingly abstract forms. Bruner also recommends the promotion of *discovery learning*, or, as it is sometimes called, *inquiry training*. In discovery learning, the teacher provides a scaffolding of experiences for the learner to climb. From participation in these experiences, students acquire an understanding of concepts and principles that is based on their personal discoveries. These three levels are used as students progress through the activities in this book. Students first directly manipulate objects such as crayons and cutouts, then manipulate mental images of those objects, and, finally, in drawing tree diagrams, manipulate symbols.

Researchers are clearly influenced by a recent psychological theory known as *constructivism*. This theory no longer views students as "passive absorbers of information, storing it in easily retrievable fragments as a result of repeated practice and enforcement." Constructivists contend that "individuals approach each new task with prior knowledge, assimilate new information, and construct their own meanings" (NCTM 1987, 8). The activities in this book are designed to provide students with the opportunity to approach each new task with prior knowledge, assimilate new information, and construct their own meanings.

The curriculum and assessment components of this book have been field-tested by classroom teachers and are correlated to mathematics curriculum and evaluation standards developed by an NCTM committee as a teaching model for students K-8. Published by NCTM in 1989, these standards generally have been accepted as the guidelines for instruction and evaluation in curriculum development. The appendix lists the standards pertaining to probability and statistics. Titles of other research on mathematics education can be found in the list of references.

The curriculum components of this book include a letter to the parent explaining the program and a pre-program parent survey. A student self-assessment handout to be used prior to beginning the program also is provided. The activity section includes a teacher guide, reproducible student activity handouts, reproducible cutout handouts of manipulatives, answer keys, and a glossary with in-depth explanations of probability and statistics terms. The materials required for the activities can easily be found in the classroom or at home. They include: paper, writing utensils, plastic lids, crayons, scissors, drinking straws, brass fasteners, markers, and Ziploc® bags or envelopes. The appendix contains a list of materials and suggestions for creating three-dimensional manipulatives. Many activities provide opportunities for students to use calculators. Calculator use is encouraged by NCTM standards, but we leave the decision to each teacher.

The assessment portion of this book includes the following reproducible forms:

- pre-program and follow-up parent letters;

- pre-program and follow-up parent surveys;

- pre-program and follow-up student self-assessment handouts;

- an evaluation of student behavior sheet, to be used throughout the course of the program by the teacher while students are involved in completing their tasks (to allow for a more comprehensive assessment of each student, it is suggested that the teacher attempt to observe only a small segment of the class on a given day);

- a group-assessment handout, to be used by students to evaluate their group experiences;

- a certificate of accomplishment, to be awarded following the successful completion of this unit of study; and

- a student journal, which provides clear and effective means for connecting math with language arts and offers students regular opportunities to synthesize the concepts they are learning.

Chances Are provides teachers, parents, and students with ongoing documentation of what students are learning and how well they are learning it. This program is designed to be compatible with portfolio assessment. Portfolios might include such evidence as samples of computations, student reflections and self-evaluations, solutions to open-ended questions, written explanations of mathematical thinking, samples that demonstrate ability improvement in solving increasingly complex word problems, and anecdotal teacher observations of student activities and interactions.

We believe that this book contains comprehensive and effective means for teaching probability and statistics. Your comments and suggestions are welcomed. The authors may be contacted in care of Berne-Knox-Westerlo Schools, 2021 Helderberg Trail, Berne, NY 12023.

Sheila Dolgowich
Helen M. Lounsbury
Barry G. Muldoon

How to Use This Book

Chances Are is teacher-friendly. It has been written by teachers, for teachers. The 13 activities in this book provide a variety of experiences designed to lead students through the fundamentals of probability and statistics. These activities may be used to supplement your mathematics program.

Each activity includes a teacher's guide; reproducible student activity handouts; sheets of cutout manipulatives, where necessary (suggestions for making a permanent set of manipulatives are included in the appendix); and an answer key, where necessary. It is recommended that activities be copied on colored paper and be kept in student portfolios. Manipulatives should be stored in separate, labeled Ziploc® bags that indicate the number of the activity and the type and quantity of the manipulatives.

Each teacher's guide includes

- the objective of the activity, always stemming from NCTM recommendations (see the appendix);

- requirements for prior knowledge;

- the estimated time needed to complete each activity;

- a list of materials that each student needs;

- recommended groupings of students;

- a list of new vocabulary terms that are introduced with the activity and defined in the glossary (not all activities have new vocabulary);

- directions for using the activity;

- suggested class-discussion questions for the analysis of outcomes (answers in parentheses follow some questions);

- recommended assessment tools, always based on NCTM suggestions; and

- suggestions for extensions of the activity.

When you are ready to begin this study of probability and statistics, the following steps are recommended:

1. Send home pre-program parent letters (page 85) and pre-program attitude surveys (page 86). You may wish to include copies of the letters and the returned surveys in students' portfolios.

2. In class, have students complete pre-program self-assessment handouts (page 87). You may wish to include these in students' portfolios.

3. Introduce *Chances Are*. Ascertain and discuss students' prior knowledge of probability and statistics. Explain how this unit of study will be "hands-on"—students will be using manipulatives to discover new strategies and concepts. Draw students' attention to SAM the mouse, who serves as a mascot for this program; point out that his name is an acronym for **S**ense-**A**ble **M**ath and that SAM and his family will be found throughout the unit. You may wish to have students make a folder or portfolio in which to keep completed activities and materials (this really comes in handy at parent-teacher conferences).

4. At the beginning of each activity, verify that each student has the necessary activity handouts, cutouts, and other materials; group students appropriately (as recommended in each teacher's guide); and follow the directions that are provided.

5. During the analysis of outcomes of each activity, establish an atmosphere that encourages a free exchange of ideas. Focus the discussion. Questions are provided specifically to help accomplish this. Encourage students to use strategies such as acting out the problem; drawing a diagram or picture; making a chart, list, or graph; and so on.

6. During the assessment of each activity, make use of the student journal (page 96), including the cover page. Journal entries are correlated to each activity. It is suggested that each student be provided with a copy of the entire journal at the beginning of this unit of study. You may wish to provide plastic covers for the journals. Become familiar with the other useful forms included in the assessment portion of this book. Also, during each activity, make use of student behavior evaluation sheets (page 89). Have students fill out group-assessment handouts (page 90) throughout the unit, where appropriate.

7. At the end of this program, send home follow-up parent letters (page 91) and follow-up surveys (page 92); on each follow-up survey, place a checkmark on the math ability scale to indicate the parent's pre-program response. Have students complete follow-up self-assessment handouts (page 93); on each follow-up self-assessment handout, place a checkmark on the math ability scale to indicate the student's pre-program response. Award each student a certificate of accomplishment (page 95).

One of the most fundamental concepts in probability is that of *sample space*. Before one can discuss the probability that a six will appear when a die is tossed, it is necessary to know about the die. How many sides does it have? (Though most people think of a die as being six-sided, many games use a die other than a cube.) What label is on each side? (More than one side could have a six.) The set of all possible results is known as the sample space.

The first few activities are designed to allow students to develop a concept of sample space. In SAM's Crayon Craziness, students discover the different ways a row of three boxes can be colored using two crayons. In analyzing with students the results of this activity, the teacher leads them into some intuitive investigation of probability by using the sample spaces students have developed.

Traffic Stopper also involves students in creating a sample space and using it as a basis for a probability experiment. The sample space for this activity is different than that for the first activity. In the first activity, a single color may be used in all of three boxes; but this activity does not allow a color to be repeated.

Creative Creatures introduces yet another type of sample space. Each of the first three activities involves filling three locations (three boxes, three lights, or three body parts). In the first activity, either of two crayons may be used to color each of three boxes; in the second activity, the stoplight lenses may be colored in any order. But in this activity, each of the three locations to be filled is unique, and each location (head, body, feet) has unique choices for that location.

Generating sample spaces in these first three activities should lead students to develop some type of strategy for finding the possible arrangements. Menu Madness gives students a much larger sample space to discover. It also gives the teacher an opportunity to discuss the terms *permutation* and *combination*. Students are instructed to make as many different menu items as they can (consisting of layers of three ingredients) and are instructed that the order in which the items are used is significant. For example, in the burger activity, the instructions say that "a burger-tomato-onion sandwich is different from an onion-burger-tomato sandwich." A distinction is made in formal probability between arrangements in which order is important and those in which it is not. A permutation is an arrangement in which the order is important. The menu activity asks students to discover the 27 different permutations of the given ingredients. A combination is an arrangement in which the order is not important. In the menu activity, there are only 10 combinations.

It's a Wrap! requires students to use a menu (generated in activity 4) to answer questions on probability. The sample space is provided; students must begin understanding the concept of the probability of an event.

Students use manipulatives to discover the possible outfits in Dressing up Probability.

A new strategy, the tree diagram, introduces students to the use of symbols rather than manipulatives to generate a sample space. Painter's Cap Possibilities is designed to provide an opportunity for the use of this new strategy, as are SAM and Samantha's Family Tree and See How They Run.

Probability Spin-Off and Qwerty Questions give students the opportunity to conduct an experiment and collect and analyze the empirical results.

Practice in compiling and organizing data is provided in Peeking at Presidents. Students are asked to present their results in both chart and graphic form. These skills are again used in Poll Cats when students are asked to formulate a question and conduct a survey.

SAM's Crayon Craziness

Teacher's Guide

Objective: Students will construct a sample space and explore the concepts of chance.

Prior Knowledge: None.

Time: One class period.

Materials: Activity handout (1) and crayons.

Grouping: Individuals or learning pairs.

New Vocabulary: Experiment, outcome, permutation, sample space, probability of an event.

Directions:

1. Designate learning pairs (optional).

2. Distrubute copies of the activity handout: SAM's Crayon Craziness.

3. Have each child select two crayons (different colors).

4. Review instructions with students while modeling the process on the chalkboard. Draw and color in an example row of boxes.

5. Give students time to complete their task.

6. Analysis of outcomes (see below).

7. Have students complete their journal entry for this activity.

8. Have volunteers share their journal responses and reactions to other's responses.

Analysis of Outcomes:

The following questions may be used to focus class discussion, reinforce new vocabulary, and extend understandings:

- How many ways did you find to color the boxes?

- What strategy did you use to complete the table? (Starting with just one color, then changing the color of one box at a time; hit and miss; and so on.) The purpose of this question is to encourage students to become aware of and implement strategies in problem solving.

- Compare your table to another student's table. Does the choice of colors affect the number of ways the chart can be colored? (No, it is the *number* of colors, not the *choice* of colors, that determines the number of permutations.)

- How many of the eight rows have all three boxes the same color? (2)

- Imagine the eight rows being cut out separately and put into a box. What do you think the chance is of reaching in, without looking, and pulling out a row that is all one color? (2/8, or 1/4, because there are two single-color rows out of a total of eight rows.) The purpose of this question is to make students aware of the basic concept underlying probability: the probability of an event is determined by the number of successful outcomes over the total number of possible outcomes.

Assessment:

- Journal entries

- Evaluating Student Behavior sheets

- Evaluation of responses during discussion

- Group Assessment handouts

* * * * *

Emphasize the vocabulary terms *experiment, outcome, permutation, sample space*, and *probability of an event* when summarizing the results of this activity. Review the strategies used by students. Demonstrate how the multiplication principle of probability can be used to determine the number of permutations. Students have two choices for the first box, two choices for the second box, and two choices for the third box, so there are 2 x 2 x 2 = 8 arrangements of colors in the boxes.

Box 1		Box 2		Box 3		
2 choices		2 choices		2 choices		
2	x	2	x	2	=	8

Extension:

Ask students to calculate how many rows would be needed to show all the ways to color the three boxes if they were to use three colors. (There are 3 x 3 x 3 = 27 arrangements.)

Ask students to calculate how many rows would be needed to show all the ways to color the three boxes if they were to use four colors. (There are 4 x 4 x 4 = 64 arrangements.)

SAM's Crayon Craziness

Choose two crayons of different colors. SAM chose a red and a green crayon. Using only those two crayons, SAM discovered eight different ways to color a row of three boxes. One of SAM's rows looked like this:

red	green	red

Now use your crayons to color each of the rows below in a different way. How many different ways can you color a row of boxes?

Answer Key
SAM's Crayon Craziness

Choose two crayons of different colors. SAM chose a red and a green crayon. Using only those two crayons, SAM discovered eight different ways to color a row of three boxes. One of SAM's rows looked like this:

red	green	red

Now use your crayons to color each of the rows below in a different way. How many different ways can you color a row of boxes? **No additional rows are needed.**

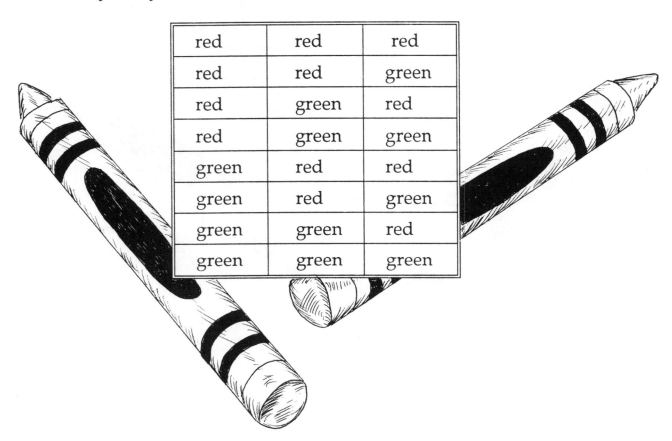

red	red	red
red	red	green
red	green	red
red	green	green
green	red	red
green	red	green
green	green	red
green	green	green

Activity 2

Traffic Stopper

Teacher's Guide

Objective: Students will construct a sample space and explore the concepts of chance.

Prior Knowledge: Students should be able to implement problem-solving strategies gained from activity 1.

Time: One class period.

Materials: Activity handouts (3), crayons, scissors.

Grouping: Individuals or learning pairs.

Directions:

1. Designate learning pairs (optional).

2. Distribute copies of the activity handouts: Traffic Stopper, Traffic Light, and Traffic Stopper Lens Cutouts.

3. Give students time to color and cut out the lenses.

4. Review instructions with students while modeling the process on the chalkboard. Draw a traffic light, choose three example colors, and label the three positions (e.g., *R* for red, *Y* for yellow, and *G* for green).

5. Give students time to complete their task.

6. Analysis of outcomes (see below).

7. Have students complete their journal entry for this activity.

8. Have volunteers share their journal responses and reactions to other's responses.

Analysis of Outcomes:

The following questions may be used to focus class discussion and extend understandings:

- How many ways did you find to color the traffic light? (6)

- What strategy did you use to complete the table?

- Compare this table to the SAM's Crayon Craziness table in activity 1. What is different about this activity? (Because each color can only be used once in the arrangement, there will not be traffic lights with two or three lights of the same color—there are fewer outcomes.)

Assessment:

- Journal entries

- Evaluating Student Behavior sheets

- Evaluation of responses during discussion

- Group Assessment handouts

* * * * *

Emphasize again the vocabulary terms *experiment, outcome, permutation, sample space,* and *probability of an event* when summarizing the results of this activity. Review the strategies used by students. Demonstrate how the multiplication principle of probability can be used to determine the number of permutations. Students have three colors to choose from for the top light. Once the top color is selected, only two color choices remain for the middle light. After the middle light's color is selected, only one color choice is left for the bottom light. There are 3 x 2 x 1 = 6 arrangements of colors in the traffic light.

Emphasize the difference between SAM's Crayon Craziness (activity 1) and this activity. In SAM's Crayon Craziness, each color could be used more than once; in this activity, repetition is not allowed.

Extension:

Ask students to calculate how many rows would be needed to show all the ways to color the three boxes, without repetition, if they were to use four colors. (There are 24 arrangements.)

Ask students if it would be possible to color a row of three boxes with only two colors if repetition were not allowed? (No, because there would be two choices for the first box, leaving only one choice for the second box, and none for the third box.)

Traffic Stopper

   Imagine you are redesigning a traffic light. Cut out the three lenses for the traffic light. Now choose three different colors for the lenses. Color the lenses. Arrange the three lenses on the traffic light. Record your first design in the table below. Now continue to rearrange the colored lenses and record the designs until you think you have recorded all possible arrangements. Add more rows as you need them.

Top Light	Center Light	Bottom Light

Use your table to answer the following questions:

1. How many arrangements of the three lenses did you discover?

2. Suppose one of each of the traffic lights that you have designed is manufactured, put into a box, and stored in a warehouse on a shelf. One day you walk into the warehouse and take one box off the shelf. What is the probability that you chose the box that contains your favorite light?

Traffic Stopper Lens Cutouts

Traffic Light

(not a cutout)

Answer Key
Traffic Stopper

Imagine you are redesigning a traffic light. Cut out the three lenses for the traffic light. Now choose three different colors for the lenses. Color the lenses. Arrange the three lenses on the traffic light. Record your first design in the table below. Now continue to rearrange the colored lenses and record the designs until you think you have recorded all possible arrangements. Add more rows as you need them.

If the student chose the colors red, pink, and blue:

Top Light	Center Light	Bottom Light
red	pink	blue
red	blue	pink
pink	red	blue
pink	blue	red
blue	pink	red
blue	red	pink

Use your table to answer the following questions:

1. How many arrangements of the three lenses did you discover? **6**

2. Suppose one of each of the traffic lights that you have designed is manufactured, put into a box, and stored in a warehouse on a shelf. One day you walk into the warehouse and take one box off the shelf. What is the probability that you chose the box that contains your favorite light? **1/6**.

Activity 3

Creative Creatures

Teacher's Guide

Objective: Students will use manipulatives to generate a sample space.

Prior Knowledge: Students should be able to implement problem-solving strategies gained from generating the sample spaces in activities 1 and 2.

Time: One class period.

Materials: Activity handouts (2), scissors, pencils.

Grouping: Learning pairs.

Directions:

1. Designate learning pairs.

2. Distribute copies of the activity handouts: Creative Creatures and Creative Creatures Cutouts.

3. Give students time to cut out the creature.

4. Review instructions with students while modeling the process on the chalkboard. Draw and fill in with body-part codes an example row of three boxes. Make sure students understand that they are to choose two head boxes, two body boxes, and two leg boxes.

5. Give students time to complete their task.

6. Analysis of outcomes (see below).

7. Have students complete their journal entry for this activity.

8. Have volunteers share their journal responses and reactions to other's responses.

Analysis of Outcomes:

The following questions may be used to focus class discussion and extend understandings:

- Using two head, two body, and two leg boxes, how many different creatures did you create? (8)

13

- What strategy did you use to complete the table?

- Compare this table to the tables in SAM's Crayon Craziness and Traffic Stopper. What is different about this activity? (The choices for heads, bodies, and legs can only be used in certain positions; that is, you cannot put a head in a leg position—there are fewer outcomes.)

Assessment:

- Journal entries

- Evaluating Student Behavior sheets

- Evaluation of responses during discussion

- Group Assessment handouts

* * * * *

Review the multiplication principle of probability when summarizing the results of this activity. There are two choices for the head, two choices for the body, and two choices for the legs, so there are 2 x 2 x 2 = 8 creatures.

Extension:

Have students vary the choices. For example, students may use all three heads, all three bodies, and all three legs to create monsters, in which case there are 3 x 3 x 3 = 27 creatures.

Ask students to design their own creature cutouts to use as additional manipulatives.

For language arts, have students write descriptions, stories, or poems about their favorite creatures.

Creative Creatures

SAM's toy factory purchases creature parts. A head, a body, and a set of legs must then be put together to form a creature. Choose any two head boxes, two body boxes, and two leg boxes. Use these parts to create as many different creatures as possible. As you make each creature, record the parts used in the table. Add more rows as you need them.

Head	Body	Legs

How many creatures did you create?

Creative Creatures Cutouts

Answer Key
Creative Creatures

SAM's toy factory purchases creature parts. A head, a body, and a set of legs must then be put together to form a creature. Choose any two head boxes, two body boxes, and two leg boxes. Use these parts to create as many different creatures as possible. As you make each creature, record the parts used in the table. Add more rows as you need them.

Head	Body	Legs
H1	B1	L1
H1	B1	L2
H1	B2	L1
H1	B2	L2
H2	B1	L1
H2	B1	L2
H2	B2	L1
H2	B2	L2

How many creatures did you create? **8**

Activity 4

Menu Madness
(SAMburgers, Deli SAMwiches, Ben & Cherries)

Teacher's Guide

Objective: Students will use manipulatives to construct a sample space for a real-world problem.

Prior Knowledge: Students will be able to apply a systematic approach to generating a sample space.

Time: Two class periods.

Materials: Activity handouts (3 for each), crayons, pencils, scissors, group assessment handouts (page 90).

Grouping: Divide the class into three task groups. Within each task group, allow students to choose a learning partner. Each task group will be assigned one of the three activities. For example, learning partners in task group one might be assigned SAMburgers, while those in task group two are assigned Deli SAMwiches and those in task group three are assigned Ben & Cherries.

Directions:

1. Designate groups.

2. Distribute copies of the activity handouts.

   For SAMburgers: SAMburgers, SAMburgers Menu, and SAMburgers Cutouts. (See page 21.)

   For Deli SAMwiches: Deli SAMwiches, Deli SAMwiches Menu, and Deli SAMwiches Cutouts. (See page 26.)

   For Ben & Cherries: Ben & Cherries, Ben & Cherries Menu, and Ben & Cherries Cutouts. (See page 31.)

3. Give students time for coloring and cutting. You may wish to provide labeled envelopes or Ziploc® bags for storage of the manipulatives.

4. In each group, review instructions with students while modeling their process on the chalkboard.

5. Give students time to complete their task.

6. Have learning pairs meet within their task groups to combine and assess results. Once the results have been finalized, have each group select a spokesperson(s) and report their findings to the class.

7. Analysis of outcomes (see below).

8. Have students complete their journal entry and group assessment handouts for this activity.

9. Have volunteers share their journal responses and reactions to other's responses.

Analysis of Outcomes:

Much of the analysis may be covered during the group presentations. The purpose of this discussion should be to link the activities. The following questions may be used to focus class discussion and extend understandings:

- How did the three activities differ? (Each involved a different product.)

- What similarities do you see in SAMburgers, Deli SAMwiches, and Ben & Cherries? (All involve arrangements, or permutations, of three ingredients.)

- What are the names of the SAMburgers, SAMwiches, and ice cream cones that you created?

Assessment:

- Journal entries

- Evaluating Student Behavior sheets

- Evaluation of responses during discussion

- Group Assessment handouts

* * * * *

Review the vocabulary terms *experiment, outcome, permutation, sample space,* and *probability of an event* when summarizing the results of this activity. Students should see the connection between the menus they have completed and the 27 possible permutations each of SAMburgers, SAMwiches, and ice cream cones. If students did not use a systematic method for completing the charts, point out that there is one. For example, in Ben & Cherries, one method would be to choose one flavor for the bottom scoop, the same flavor for the middle scoop, and then exhaust all possibilities for the third scoop:

    cherry–cherry–*cherry*
    cherry–cherry–*vanilla*
    cherry–cherry–*blueberry*

Next, change the middle scoop and again exhaust all possibilities for the third scoop:

    cherry–*vanilla–cherry*
    cherry–*vanilla–vanilla*
    cherry–*vanilla–blueberry*

Once again, change the middle scoop and exhaust all possibilities for the third scoop:

    cherry–*blueberry–cherry*
    cherry–*blueberry–vanilla*
    cherry–*blueberry–blueberry*

Now, change the bottom scoop and repeat the above process. Finally, change the bottom scoop again and repeat the above process once more.

Extension:

Have students work with one of the other menu activities, either as a follow-up, or as an opportunity for further practice.

SAMburgers

How many different SAMburgers can you offer if each SAMburger has *exactly* three items (choose from burgers, tomatoes, and onions) inside a bun? Keep track of all the SAMburgers you make on the SAMburgers Menu handout. Make up names for some. *(Hint: Make an onion-onion-onion SAMburger; it's called a Bad-Breath Special!)*

Note: A burger-tomato-onion SAMburger is different than an onion-burger-tomato SAMburger.

SAMburgers Menu

Bottom Item	Middle Item	Top Item

SAMburgers Cutouts

Answer Key
SAMburgers

Bottom Item	Middle Item	Top Item
burger	burger	burger
burger	burger	tomato
burger	burger	onion
burger	tomato	burger
burger	tomato	tomato
burger	tomato	onion
burger	onion	burger
burger	onion	tomato
burger	onion	onion
tomato	burger	burger
tomato	burger	tomato
tomato	burger	onion
tomato	tomato	burger
tomato	tomato	tomato
tomato	tomato	onion
tomato	onion	burger
tomato	onion	tomato
tomato	onion	onion
onion	burger	burger
onion	burger	tomato
onion	burger	onion
onion	tomato	burger
onion	tomato	tomato
onion	tomato	onion
onion	onion	burger
onion	onion	tomato
onion	onion	onion

Deli SAMwiches

How many different SAMwiches can you make with the ingredients provided (choose from bacon, lettuce, and cheese) if each SAMwich has *exactly* three ingredients? Keep track of your results on the Deli SAMwich Menu handout. Try to make up deli names for some of the SAMwiches. (Hint: *Make a Three Little Pigs bacon-bacon-bacon SAMwich!*)

Note: A bacon-lettuce-lettuce SAMwich is different from lettuce-bacon-lettuce SAMwich!

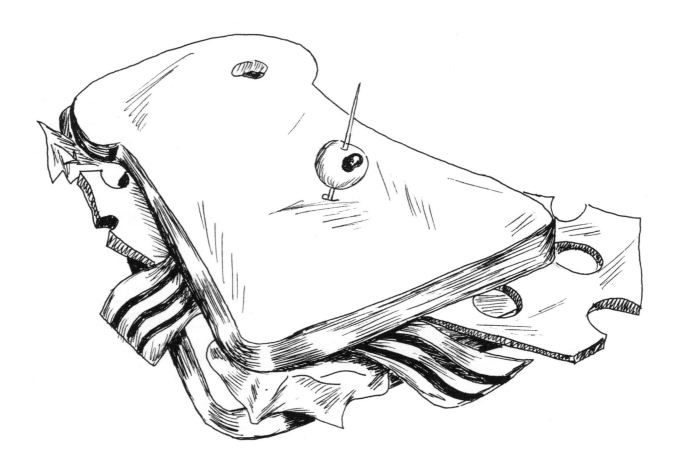

Deli SAMwiches Menu

Bottom Item	Middle Item	Top Item

From *Chances Are.* © 1995. Teacher Ideas Press, P.O. Box 6633, Englewood, CO 80155-6633. 1-800-237-6124.

Deli SAMwiches Cutouts

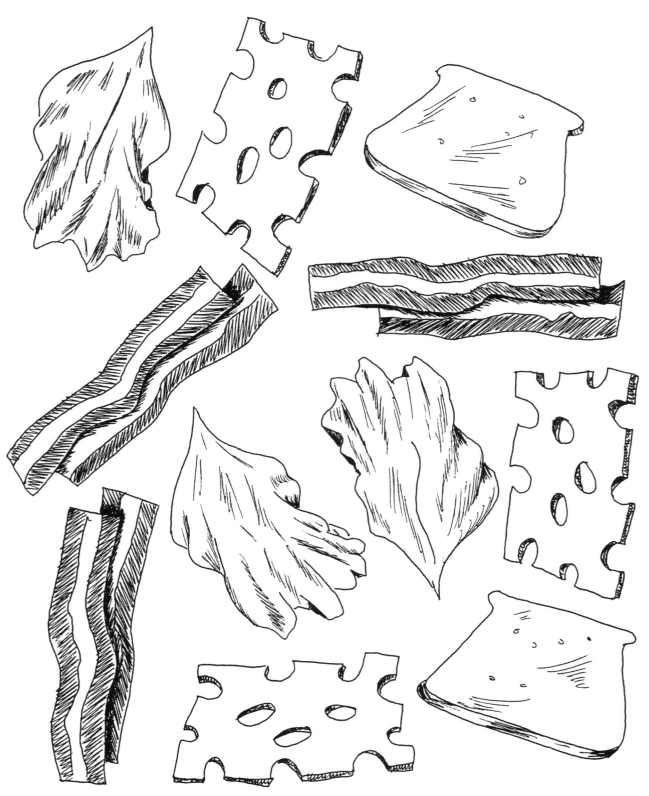

Answer Key
Deli SAMwiches

Bottom Item	Middle Item	Top Item
Lettuce	Lettuce	Lettuce
Lettuce	Lettuce	Bacon
Lettuce	Lettuce	Cheese
Lettuce	Bacon	Lettuce
Lettuce	Bacon	Bacon
Lettuce	Bacon	Cheese
Lettuce	Cheese	Lettuce
Lettuce	Cheese	Bacon
Lettuce	Cheese	Cheese
Bacon	Lettuce	Lettuce
Bacon	Lettuce	Bacon
Bacon	Lettuce	Cheese
Bacon	Bacon	Lettuce
Bacon	Bacon	Bacon
Bacon	Bacon	Cheese
Bacon	Cheese	Lettuce
Bacon	Cheese	Bacon
Bacon	Cheese	Cheese
Cheese	Lettuce	Lettuce
Cheese	Lettuce	Bacon
Cheese	Lettuce	Cheese
Cheese	Bacon	Lettuce
Cheese	Bacon	Bacon
Cheese	Bacon	Cheese
Cheese	Cheese	Lettuce
Cheese	Cheese	Bacon
Cheese	Cheese	Cheese

Ben & Cherries

How many different three-scoop cones can you make using red scoops, blue scoops, and white scoops. Keep track of the cones you make on the Ben & Cherries Menu handout? Make up names for some of your cones. (Hint: *Make a cherry-vanilla-blueberry cone; it's called a Flag-Waver!*)

Note: A cherry-vanilla-blueberry cone is different than a vanilla-blueberry-cherry cone.

From *Chances Are.* © 1995. Teacher Ideas Press, P.O. Box 6633, Englewood, CO 80155-6633. 1-800-237-6124.

Ben & Cherries Menu

Bottom Scoop	Middle Scoop	Top Scoop

Ben & Cherries Cutouts

Answer Key
Ben & Cherries

Bottom Scoop	Middle Scoop	Top Scoop
Cherry	Cherry	Cherry
Cherry	Cherry	Vanilla
Cherry	Cherry	Blueberry
Cherry	Vanilla	Cherry
Cherry	Vanilla	Vanilla
Cherry	Vanilla	Blueberry
Cherry	Blueberry	Cherry
Cherry	Blueberry	Vanilla
Cherry	Blueberry	Blueberry
Vanilla	Cherry	Cherry
Vanilla	Cherry	Vanilla
Vanilla	Cherry	Blueberry
Vanilla	Vanilla	Cherry
Vanilla	Vanilla	Vanilla
Vanilla	Vanilla	Blueberry
Vanilla	Blueberry	Cherry
Vanilla	Blueberry	Vanilla
Vanilla	Blueberry	Blueberry
Blueberry	Cherry	Cherry
Blueberry	Cherry	Vanilla
Blueberry	Cherry	Blueberry
Blueberry	Vanilla	Cherry
Blueberry	Vanilla	Vanilla
Blueberry	Vanilla	Blueberry
Blueberry	Blueberry	Cherry
Blueberry	Blueberry	Vanilla
Blueberry	Blueberry	Blueberry

It's a Wrap!

Teacher's Guide

Objective: Students will determine the probability of a specific real-world event using a previously generated sample space.

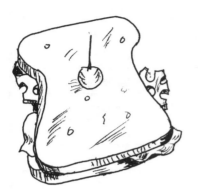

Prior Knowledge: Students must know that the probability of a particular event is a number between 0 and 1 inclusive, and that the probability of a particular event can be found by forming the fraction:

$$\frac{\text{number of outcomes satisfying condition}}{\text{number of outcomes in sample space}}$$

This concept can easily be taught using the Deli SAMwiches Menu. For example, the probability of getting a sandwich with cheese as the middle item is 9/27, or 1/3 in reduced form (the menu chart shows that 9 of the 27 sandwiches have cheese listed as the middle item). The probability of getting a sandwich containing peanut butter is 0, because no (0 out of 27) sandwiches in the sample space contain peanut butter. The probability of getting a sandwich that contains bread is 1 because all sandwiches (27 out of 27) are made with bread.

Time: One class period.

Materials: Activity handouts (2), pencils.

Grouping: Learning pairs.

New Vocabulary: Probability of an event.

Directions:

1. Designate learning pairs.

2. Distribute copies of the activity handouts: It's a Wrap and Deli SAMwiches Menu.

3. Review instructions with students and present the lesson and examples in "Prior Knowledge," above.

4. Give students time to complete their task. The teacher should use the Evaluating Student Behavior sheet (see page 89) to record observations of students.

5. Analysis of outcomes (see below).

6. Have students complete their journal entry for this activity.

7. Have volunteers share their journal responses and reactions to other's responses.

Analysis of Outcomes:

The purpose of this discussion should be to verify student responses and to allow students to verbalize the methods used to arrive at the probability of each event. The following questions may be used to focus class discussion, reinforce new vocabulary, and extend understandings:

- What is your answer to question number ___ ?

- What strategy did you use to arrive at that answer?

- How do you justify your response?

- Have you learned different strategies from your classmates?

Assessment:

- Journal entries

- Evaluating Student Behavior sheets

- Evaluation of responses during discussion

- Group Assessment handouts

* * * * *

After summarizing the results of this activity, if students are familiar with percents, explain that probability can be given as a percent between 0% and 100%. For this example, the answer 9/27 could also be expressed as 33-1/3%. This is often the case in weather prediction, for instance: discuss with students what it means if the "probability of precipitation" is 80%. Should they schedule a picnic?

Extension:

Encourage students to keep a log of weather reports and to relate the reports to what they have learned about the probability of an event.

It's A Wrap!

You are going on a picnic with a group of students. They order a box of sandwiches from Deli SAMwiches. The box contains one of each of the 27 different types of sandwiches listed on the Deli SAMwiches menu. You will get to reach into the box and choose any sandwich—*but* the sandwiches are all wrapped in plain white paper and they are not marked!

Use your menu to answer the following questions:

1. What is the probability that you will choose a bacon-bacon-bacon sandwich?

2. What is the probability that you will choose a bacon-cheese-bacon sandwich?

3. What is the probability that the sandwich you choose will have lettuce as the bottom item?

4. What is the probability that the sandwich you choose will have bacon as the middle item?

5. What is the probability that the sandwich you choose will have cheese as the middle item?

6. What is the probability that the sandwich you choose will have *exactly* two pieces of lettuce in it? *At least* two pieces?

7. What is the probability that the sandwich you choose will have *exactly* one piece of bacon in it?

8. What is the probability that the sandwich you choose will *not* have cheese in it?

From *Chances Are.* © 1995. Teacher Ideas Press, P.O. Box 6633, Englewood, CO 80155-6633. 1-800-237-6124.

Deli SAMwiches Menu

Bottom Item	Middle Item	Top Item
Lettuce	Lettuce	Lettuce
Lettuce	Lettuce	Bacon
Lettuce	Lettuce	Cheese
Lettuce	Bacon	Lettuce
Lettuce	Bacon	Bacon
Lettuce	Bacon	Cheese
Lettuce	Cheese	Lettuce
Lettuce	Cheese	Bacon
Lettuce	Cheese	Cheese
Bacon	Lettuce	Lettuce
Bacon	Lettuce	Bacon
Bacon	Lettuce	Cheese
Bacon	Bacon	Lettuce
Bacon	Bacon	Bacon
Bacon	Bacon	Cheese
Bacon	Cheese	Lettuce
Bacon	Cheese	Bacon
Bacon	Cheese	Cheese
Cheese	Lettuce	Lettuce
Cheese	Lettuce	Bacon
Cheese	Lettuce	Cheese
Cheese	Bacon	Lettuce
Cheese	Bacon	Bacon
Cheese	Bacon	Cheese
Cheese	Cheese	Lettuce
Cheese	Cheese	Bacon
Cheese	Cheese	Cheese

Answer Key
It's a Wrap!

You are going on a picnic with a group of students. They order a box of sandwiches from Deli SAMwiches. The box contains one of each of the 27 different types of sandwiches listed on the Deli SAMwiches menu. You will get to reach into the box and choose any sandwich—*but* the sandwiches are all wrapped in plain white paper and they are not marked!

Use your menu to answer the following questions:

1. What is the probability that you will choose a bacon-bacon-bacon sandwich? **1/27**

2. What is the probability that you will choose a bacon-cheese-bacon sandwich? **1/27**

3. What is the probability that the sandwich you choose will have lettuce as the bottom item? **9/27, or 1/3**

4. What is the probability that the sandwich you choose will have bacon as the middle item? **9/27, or 1/3**

5. What is the probability that the sandwich you choose will have cheese as the middle item? **9/27, or 1/3**

6. What is the probability that the sandwich you choose will have *exactly* two pieces of lettuce in it? *At least* two pieces? **exactly = 6/27, or 2/9; at least = 7/27**

7. What is the probability that the sandwich you choose will have *exactly* one piece of bacon in it? **12/27, or 4/9**

8. What is the probability that the sandwich you choose will *not* have cheese in it? **8/27**

Activity 6

Dressing up Probability

Teacher's Guide

Objective: Students will practice using manipulatives to generate a sample space; students will use the sample space to find probabilities of events. Tree diagrams, a new strategy, will be introduced as a means of organizing and describing data.

Prior Knowledge: Students should understand how to find the probability of an event.

Time: One class period.

Materials: Activity handouts (2), Dressing up Probability Chalkboard Cutouts (2), crayons, pencils, scissors.

Grouping: Learning pairs.

New Vocabulary: Event, tree diagram.

Directions:

1. Make four copies of chalkboard cutout T-shirt and four copies of the chalkboard cutout pair of shorts. Color two T-shirts and two pairs of shorts yellow; color two T-shirts and two pairs of shorts green. Cut them out and set them aside for use after the assessment.

2. Designate learning pairs.

3. Distribute copies of the activity handouts: Dressing up Probability and Dressing up Probability Cutouts.

4. Give students time to color and cut out the T-shirts and shorts.

5. Review instructions with students.

6. Give students time to complete their task.

7. Analysis of outcomes (see below).

8. Have students complete their journal entry for this activity.

9. Have volunteers share their journal responses and reactions to other's responses.

Analysis of Outcomes:

The following questions may be used to focus class discussion, reinforce new vocabulary, and extend understandings:

- What strategies did you use to generate the sample space? (Maintain one variable constant, trial and error, and so on.)

- Could you have generated the sample space without the manipulatives? (We hope so!)

- What strategies might be used to solve this problem without manipulatives? (Making lists or charts, drawing pictures, and so on.)

Ask students to share and justify their answers to the probability questions on the handout.

Assessment:

- Journal entries

- Evaluating Student Behavior sheets

- Evaluation of responses during discussion

- Group Assessment handouts

* * * * *

Emphasize the vocabulary terms *event* and *tree diagram* when summarizing the results of this activity. This is a good time to discuss a tree diagram's use for finding the sample space and in finding probability. Ask students which cutout they want to start with, shirt or shorts. If the choice is *shorts*, hang one pair of yellow shorts and one pair of green shorts on the chalkboard as shown in the diagram (if the choice is

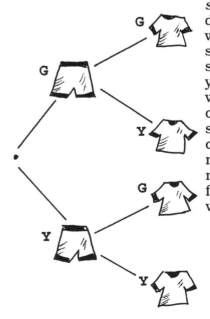

shirts, substitute shirts for shorts and vice versa in the diagram). Then ask, "If you choose to wear the green shorts, what colors of shirts could you choose to wear?" Hang two shirts (one green and one yellow) on the chalkboard as shown in the diagram. Next ask, "If you choose to wear the yellow shorts, what colors of shirts could you choose to wear?" Hang a yellow and a green shirt as shown in the diagram. Draw lines as shown between the shorts and shirts. Point out to students that this is called a tree diagram because it has "branches," or paths. Each branch represents one possible outcome, and the whole tree represents the same sample space they generated in table form. Point out that the diagram does not have to be drawn with pictures; words can be used, or the letters *y* and *g*.

Extension:

The Probability Tree for a Three-Child Family handout included with this activity provides an opportunity for students to have a hands-on introductory experience with this means of organizing and recording data. The completed tree diagram should be saved in students' portfolios. Activity 8 will ask students to extend this tree. Explain that the first child could be either a boy or a girl. Help students fill in the blank spaces in the tree by listing on the chalkboard all possible three-child families that can be shown on the tree diagram: BBB, BBG, BGB, BGG, GBB, GBG, GGB, GGG. Ask students to count the number of possible outcomes (there are 8). To further reinforce the concept of probability, ask the following questions:

- What is the probability of all three children being boys? (1/8)

- What is the probability of all three children being girls? (1/8)

- What is the probability of the oldest child being a boy? (4/8, or 1/2)

- What is the probability of the middle child being a girl? (4/8, or 1/2)

- What is the probability of having two boys and one girl, in any order? (3/8)

Dressing up Probability

Pretend you own two T-shirts (one yellow and one green) and two pairs of shorts (one yellow and one green). Use the cutouts to represent this clothing. Put together four different outfits. (Remember the multiplication principle of probability : 2 choices for the shirt x 2 choices for the shorts = 4 possible outfits.) Record the outfits you make into the table below.

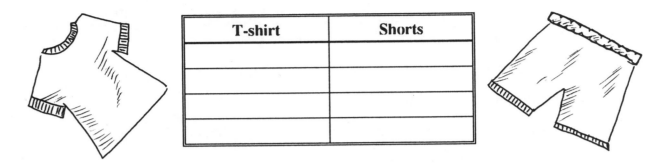

T-shirt	Shorts

You throw your two T-shirts into a pile on the right side of your bed and your two pairs of shorts into a pile on the left side. When you get up in the morning, in the dark, you grab a T-shirt and then a pair of shorts.

Use your table of outfits to answer the following questions:

1. What is the probability that you have chosen an outfit that is all one color?

2. Circle your favorite outfit on the table. What is the probability that you have chosen your favorite outfit?

3. What is the probability that you have chosen an outfit with a yellow T-shirt?

4. What is the probability that you have chosen an outfit with red shorts?

Dressing up Probability Cutouts

Dressing up Probability Chalkboard Cutouts

Dressing up Probability Chalkboard Cutouts

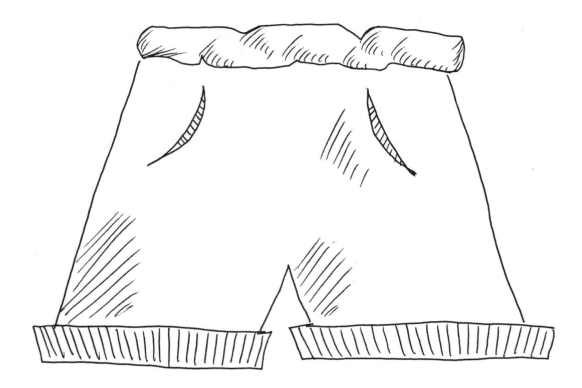

Probability Tree for a Three-Child Family
(extension)

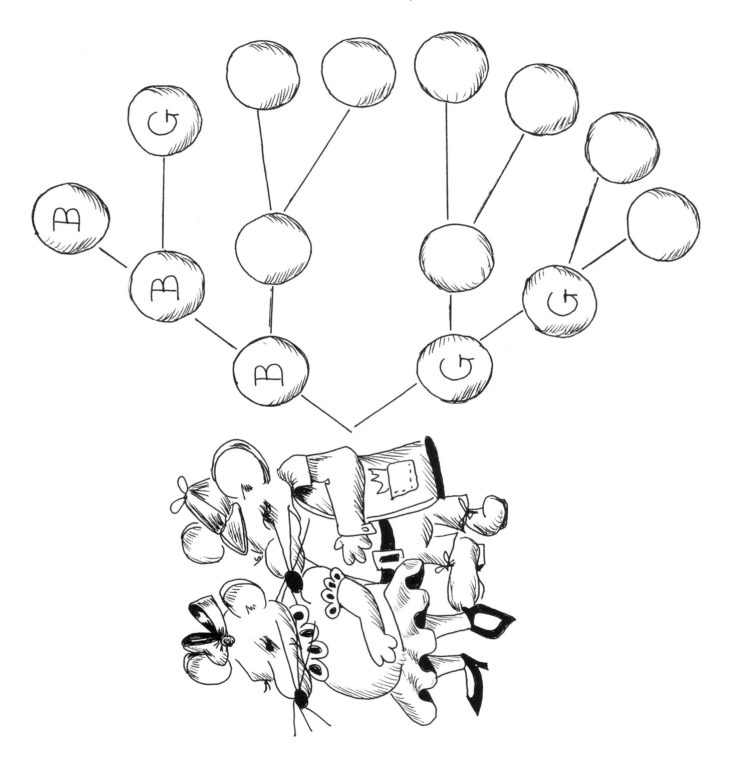

Answer Key
Dressing up Probability

Pretend you own two T-shirts (one yellow and one green) and two pairs of shorts (one yellow and one green). Use the cutouts to represent this clothing. Put together four different outfits. (Remember the multiplication principle of probability : 2 choices for the shirt x 2 choices for the shorts = 4 possible outfits.) Record the outfits you make into the table below:

T-shirt	Shorts
Green	Green
Green	Yellow
Yellow	Green
Yellow	Yellow

You throw your two T-shirts into a pile on the right side of your bed and your two pairs of shorts into a pile on the left side. When you get up in the morning, in the dark, you grab a T-shirt and then a pair of shorts.

Use your table of outfits to answer the following questions:

1. What is the probability that you have chosen an outfit that is all one color? **2/4, or 1/2**

2. Circle your favorite outfit on the table. What is the probability that you have chosen your favorite outfit? **1/4**

3. What is the probability that you have chosen an outfit with a yellow T-shirt? **2/4, or 1/2**

4. What is the probability that you have chosen an outfit with red shorts? **0**

Painter's Cap Possibilities

Teacher's Guide

Objective: Students will practice constructing, reading, and interpreting a tree diagram as a display of data.

Prior Knowledge: Students should know how to find the probability of an event, and should be familiar with a tree diagram.

Time: One class period.

Materials: Activity handout (1), pencils.

Grouping: Individuals or learning pairs.

Directions:

1. Designate learning pairs (optional).

2. Distribute copies of the activity handout: Painter's Cap Possibilities.

3. Review instructions with students.

4. Give students time to complete their task.

5. Analysis of outcomes (see below).

6. Have students complete their journal entry for this activity.

7. Have volunteers share their journal responses and reactions to other's responses.

Analysis of Outcomes:

The following questions may be used to focus class discussion and extend understandings:

*   How many branches are on your tree? (8)

*   What does that mean? (8 different outfits)

*   What did you predict for the probability that you would be wearing all one color if you picked an outfit in the dark set? (2/8, or 1/4) That your shorts and hat would be the same color? (4/8, or 1/2)

Ask students to share some of their made-up probability questions with the class and explain their answers.

Assessment:

- Journal entries

- Evaluating Student Behavior sheets

- Evaluation of responses during discussion

- Group Assessment handouts

* * * * *

After summarizing the results of this activity, post some of the painter's cap tree diagrams. Students should be aware of the fact that there are now eight paths in the diagram. Applying the multiplication principle of probability to two choices for a pair of shorts, two choices for a shirt, and two choices for a cap results in 2 x 2 x 2 = 8 outfits.

Painter's Cap Possibilities

You lucky kid! Your favorite aunt just sent you a present—two painter's caps, one green and one yellow. (She must know your outfits!) Draw a tree diagram of all the possible outfits you have now. An outfit includes a T-shirt, a pair of shorts, and a painter's cap. Remember, you have green and yellow of each item.

My Clothes Tree

Use your tree diagram to answer the following questions:

1. How many outfits do you have?

2. If you pick an outfit in the dark, what is the probability that it is all one color?

3. What is the probability that your shorts and hat are the same color?

Make up three probability questions related to this activity to share with the class. Include answers.

1.

2.

3.

Answer Key
Painter's Cap Possibilities

You lucky kid! Your favorite aunt just sent you a present—two painter's caps, one green and one yellow. (She must know your outfits!) Draw a tree diagram of all the possible outfits you have now. An outfit includes a T-shirt, a pair of shorts, and a painter's cap. Remember, you have green and yellow of each item.

My Clothes Tree

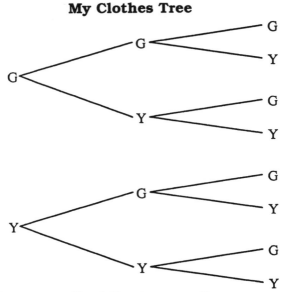

Use your tree diagram to answer the following questions:

1. How many outfits do you have? **8**

2. If you pick an outfit in the dark, what is the probability that it is all one color? **2/8, or 1/4**

3. What is the probability that your shorts and hat are the same color? **4/8, or 1/2**

SAM *and* Samantha's Family Tree

Teacher's Guide

Objective: Students will construct a tree diagram to reinforce their understanding of its potential as a display of data.

Prior Knowledge: Students should be familiar with a tree diagram.

Time: One class period.

Materials: Activity handout (1), pencils, Probability Tree for a Three-Child Family handout from activity 6.

Grouping: Individuals.

Directions:

1. Distribute copies of the activity handout: SAM and Samantha's Family Tree.

2. Review instructions with students.

3. Give students time to complete their task.

4. Analysis of outcomes (see below).

5. Have students complete their journal entry for this activity.

6. Have volunteers share their journal responses and reactions to other's responses.

Analysis of Outcomes:

The following questions may be used to focus class discussion and extend understandings:

- How many branches are in your tree? (32)

- What does that mean? (32 orders of age for a five-child family)

- What other ways might you use to show all the possible age orders for a five-child family? (Lists, charts, pictures, and so on.)

In a general summary, make sure that students have 32 branches in their family trees for SAM and Samantha. Post some of the trees.

Assessment:

- Journal entries

- Evaluating Student Behavior sheets

- Evaluation of responses during discussion

- Evaluation of student tree diagrams

* * * * *

Extension:

The names of the young mice are significant. Students should be encouraged to research and report on their origin. Have students investigate the lives of other famous mathematicians. Though the three male names are fairly well known, the female names are not, as women historically are often overlooked. In SAM's family, Hypatia's namesake was born in Athens circa 370 A.D. She taught geometry, algebra, and astronomy at Alexandria and designed variations on the astrolabe and hydroscope. Ada Lovelace, actually Ada Augusta Byron or Lady Lovelace, is regarded as the first computer programmer. She worked with Charles Babbage's Analytical Difference Machine in the 1830s. A computer programming language, Ada®, used by the U.S. Department of Defense, has been named for her.

A good source of information about notable women is *The Book of Women* by Lynne Griffen and Kelly McCann (Holbrook, MA: Bob Adams, 1992).

SAM and Samantha's Family Tree

SAM and Samantha have five children. Expand the Probability Tree for a Three-Child Family handout to show all the possible families of five children.

Use your expanded tree diagram to find

1. the number of possible five-child families:_____,

2. the number of families that have five boys:_____,

3. the number of families that have exactly one girl:_____,

4. the number of families that have at least one girl:_____, and

5. the number of families that have three boys and two girls:_____.

SAM and Samantha have three sons (Euclid, Newton, and Copernicus) and two daughters (Hypatia and Ada Lovelace). Use your answers above to answer the following questions:

6. What is the probability that a five-child family will be like SAM's (three boys and two girls)?

7. What is the probability that a five-child family will not be like SAM's?

Answer Key
SAM and Samantha's Family Tree

SAM and Samantha have five children. Expand the Probability Tree for a Three-Child Family handout to show all the possible families of five children.

Use your expanded tree diagram to find

1. the number of possible five-child families: **32** ,

2. the number of families that have five boys: **1** ,

3. the number of families that have exactly one girl: **5** ,

4. the number of families that have at least one girl: **31** , and

5. the number of families that have three boys and two girls: **10** .

SAM and Samantha have three sons (Euclid, Newton, and Copernicus) and two daughters (Hypatia and Ada Lovelace). Use your answers above to answer the following questions:

6. What is the probability that a five-child family will be like SAM's (three boys and two girls)? **10/32, or 5/16**

7. What is the probability that a five-child family will not be like SAM's? **22/32, or 11/16**

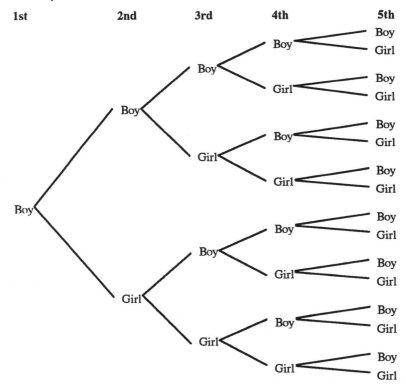

This is the top half of the tree; to form the bottom half, change the 1st child to *girl*.

Activity 9

See How They Run

Teacher's Guide

Objective: Students construct a tree diagram and use this data display to answer questions about the posssible branches in the problem.

Prior Knowledge: Students should be familiar with a tree diagram.

Time: One class period.

Materials: Activity handouts (2), pencils, crayons.

Grouping: Individuals.

Directions:

1. Distribute copies of the activity handouts: See How They Run and See How They Run Tree Diagram.

2. Review instructions with students.

3. Give students time to complete their task.

4. Analysis of outcomes (see below).

5. Have students complete their journal entry for this activity.

6. Have volunteers share their journal responses and reactions to other's responses.

Analysis of Outcomes:

The following questions may be used to focus class discussion and extend understandings:

*   How many branches are in your tree? (24)

*   Why might the order of the runners be important in a relay race?

*   What other methods might you use to show SAM's possible choices?

All students should understand that the tree should have 24 branches.

Assessment:

- Journal Entries

- Evaluating Student Behavior sheets

- Evaluation of tree diagrams

* * * * *

Extension:

Have students design their own marathon race. Have students write an eyewitness description of the race from various points of view (participant, spectator, and reporter).

See How They Run

Four of SAM's children—two girls, Hypatia and Ada; and two boys, Euclid and Newton—are planning to enter the Farmer's Wife Relay Marathon. The race is split into four parts: the Field Flee, the Yard Stick, the Porch Swing, and the Home Stretch. SAM needs to decide who will run each part of the race. On your See How They Run Tree Diagram handout, draw a tree that shows all of SAM's possible choices. For example, on the entry form, SAM might list the following lineup: Field Flee—Hypatia, Yard Stick—Euclid, Porch Swing—Newton, Home Stretch—Ada.

Use your tree to answer the following questions:

1. How many ways did you find for the team to run the race?

2. How many arrangements have Euclid running the Yard Stick part of the race?

3. How many arrangements have a girl running the Field Flee part of the race?

4. How many arrangements have a boy running both the Field Flee and the Home Stretch?

See How They Run Tree Diagram

SAM needs to decide who will run each part of the Farmer's Wife Relay Marathon. Draw a tree that shows all possible choices.

Answer Key
See How They Run

Four of SAM's children—two girls, Hypatia and Ada; and two boys, Euclid and Newton—are planning to enter the "Farmer's Wife Relay Marathon." The race is split into four parts: the Field Flee, the Yard Stick, the Porch Swing, and the Home Stretch. SAM needs to decide who will run each part of the race. On your See How They Run Tree Diagram handout, draw a tree that shows all of SAM's possible choices. For example, on the entry form, SAM might list the following lineup: Field Flee—Hypatia, Yard Stick—Euclid, Porch Swing—Newton, Home Stretch—Ada.

Use your tree to answer the following questions:

1. How many ways did you find for the team to run the race? **24**

2. How many arrangements have Euclid running the Yard Stick part of the race? **6**

3. How many arrangements have a girl running the Field Flee part of the race? **12**

4. How many arrangements have a boy running both the Field Flee and the Home Stretch? **4**

Answer Key
See How They Run Tree Diagram

The following tree diagram uses the first letter of each name (A=Ada, E=Euclid, N=Newton, H= Hypatia).

Farmer's Wife Relay Marathon

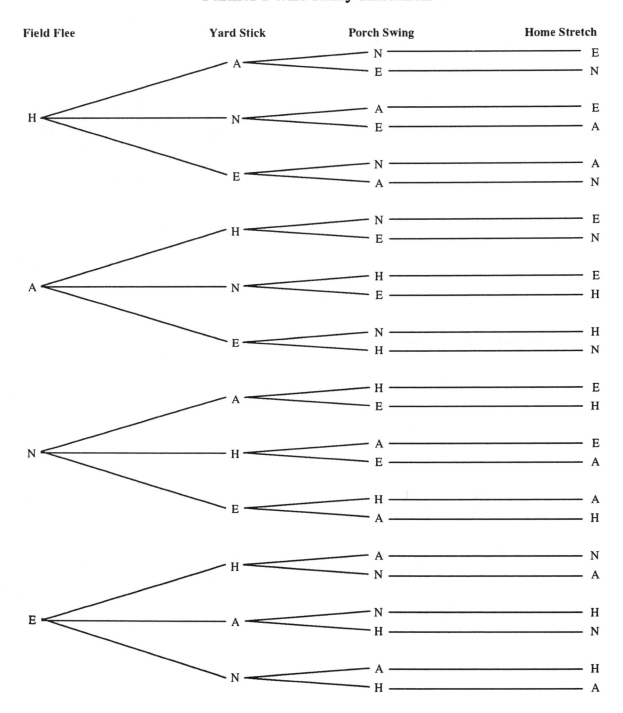

Activity 10

Probability Spin-Off

Teacher's Guide

Objective: Students will conduct an experiment and chart their results to compare *theoretical prediction* to *empirical results.*

Prior Knowledge: Students should know how to find the probability of an event.

Time: One or two class periods (two if spinners are to be constructed).

Materials: Activity handout (1), spinners, pencils.

Grouping: Learning pairs.

New Vocabulary: Empirical results, theoretical prediction.

Directions:

1. Make, or have students make, the spinners. A direction handout—Spinner Construction Instructions—is included with this activity.

2. Designate learning pairs.

3. Distribute copies of the activity handout: Probability Spin-Off.

4. Review instructions with students.

5. Give students time to complete their task.

6. Analysis of outcomes (see below).

7. Have students complete their journal entry for this activity.

8. Have volunteers share their journal responses and reactions to other's responses.

Analysis of Outcomes:

The following questions may be used to focus class discussion, reinforce new vocabulary, and extend understandings:

- What did you predict for the probability of spinning an *A*? (1/3) *B*? (1/3) *C*? (1/3)

- Did the results of your experiment agree with this prediction? That is, did you spin each possible outcome exactly 33 times?

- If not, how do you explain the fact that your results were different?

Assessment:

- Journal entries

- Evaluating Student Behavior sheets

- Evaluation of responses during discussion

* * * * *

Emphasize the vocabulary terms *empirical results* and *theoretical prediction* when summarizing the results of this activity. Make sure students understand that the probability of spinning a particular outcome is 1/3 because there are three equally likely outcomes, but this does not mean that if they spin the spinner three times it will land exactly once on each letter! Students should be able to infer that the more times they spin the spinner, the closer the number of occurences for each outcome will be to 1/3 of the total number of spins. To demonstrate this, pool the results of several pairs of students and check to see if the letter *A* came up close to 1/3 of the time, or compare the results of all pairs and find the average (mean) number of times each letter was spun.

Extension:

Change the spinner so that there are four equal sections. Color two sections red, one blue, and one green. Have students make predictions and investigate the results of spinning this spinner 100 times.

As a follow-up activity to be done either in the classroom or at home, have students flip a coin 200 times and keep a table of their results. Before beginning, they should determine the probability of a coin landing heads up and the probability of a coin landing tails up; then students should make a prediction about how many times the coin will land heads up and how many times it will land tails up.

Probability Spin-Off

1. Examine your spinner. What are the three possible outcomes of a spin?

2. Choose one outcome. What is the probability of the arrow stopping on this outcome if you spin the spinner once?

3. On the table below, predict how many times each outcome will occur if the spinner is used 99 times.

Outcome	Total

4. Now spin the spinner 99 times. Record your results as slashes into the table below.

Outcome	Tally of Occurrences	Total

5. Compare the totals from the two tables. Are they the same?_____ How do you explain this?

Spinner Construction Instructions

Materials:

Markers
Plastic drinking straws
Oaktag
Laminate or clear contact paper
Hole punch
Plastic lid (coffee can lid or similar)
Paper fasteners
Old plastic notebook binders (optional)

Procedure:

1. Cut an oaktag circle to fit into the plastic lid. Divide the lid into three equal sections and label with markers the letters *A, B,* and *C.* Laminate or cover with clear contact paper when completed.

2. Cut spinner arrow from the oaktag and either laminate or cover with clear contact paper. (If old plastic binders are available, the arrow may be cut from these.)

3. Punch a hole through the center of the arrow.

4. Cut a length of straw not more than 1/8-inch long.

5. Assemble in the following order: place the oaktag circle into plastic lid, put the straw through the arrow, slide the fastener through the straw and lid as shown, and secure fastener to the bottom of the lid.

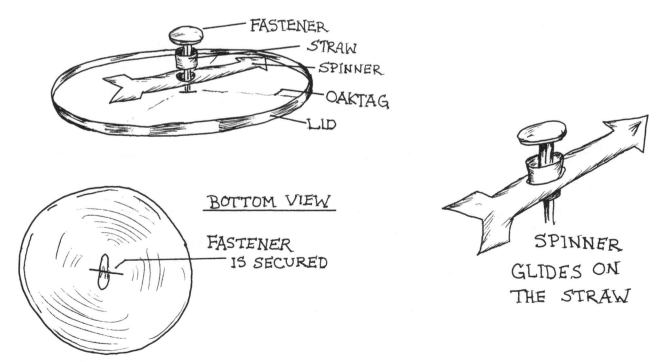

Answer Key
Probability Spin-Off

1. Examine your spinner. What are the three possible outcomes of a spin? **A, B, C**

2. Choose one outcome. What is the probability of the arrow stopping on this outcome if you spin the spinner once? **1/3**

3. On the table below, predict how many times each outcome will occur if the spinner is used 99 times.

Outcome	Total
A	33
B	33
C	33

Answers to questions 4 and 5 will vary.

Activity II

Qwerty Questions

Teacher's Guide

Objective: Students will practice compiling and organizing data.

Prior Knowledge: Students should be able to draw a chart and organize data.

Time: One class period.

Materials: Activity handouts (2), pencils, supply of paperback books.

Grouping: Learning pairs.

Directions:

1. Designate learning pairs.

2. Distribute copies of the activity handouts: Qwerty Questions and Qwerty Questions Frequency Chart.

3. Review instructions with students while modeling the process on the chalkboard: draw and fill in the "a" row of the frequency chart as an example. Use slashes in the "tally" column and an arabic numeral (that represents the number of slashes) in the "frequency" column.

4. Have students choose their paperback books. The use of textbooks in this activity is not recommended because the controlled vocabulary used in some texts may not typify standard narrative patterns, and it is the authors' belief that reading a passage from a novel may serve to inspire recreational reading.

5. Give students time to complete their task.

6. Analysis of outcomes (see below).

7. Have students complete their journal entry for this activity.

8. Have volunteers share their journal responses and reactions to other's responses.

Analysis of Outcomes:

The following questions may be used to focus class discussion and extend understanding:

- What did you predict for the letters that were used most? Why?

- What did you predict for the letters that were used least? Why?

- In the reading passage you chose, what letters were used most? Least?

- Do the results of your experiment agree with those of most of your classmates?

- If not, how do you explain this?

Assessment:

- Journal entries

- Evaluating Student Behavior sheets

- Evaluation of responses during discussion

- Group Assessment handouts

* * * * *

Extension:

After students complete activity 12, in which bar graphs are introduced, have them return to this activity and use their collected data to construct bar graphs.

Qwerty Questions

The picture below is of a standard IBM computer keyboard. The arrangement of the letters is the standard typewriter layout developed in 1872 by Christopher Sholes. In a *typewriter*, each key is connected to a striker bar, which impacts the ink ribbon against the paper, leaving a printed letter, number, or symbol. Sholes arranged the keys to prevent the striker bars of the most commonly used letters from getting jammed. Computer printers do not have striker bars, so the keys can be arranged in any fashion on the keyboard. But the arrangement of keys did not change because everyone was used to Christopher Sholes's layout. It is sometimes called the "qwerty" keyboard (from the top row of letters).

- Put an *X* through the two letter keys that you think are used most.

- Draw a circle around the two letter keys that you think are used least.

- Choose any book from the classroom reading library. Choose any page in that book.

    Start at the top of the page and count off the first 500 letters on the page.

    Count the number of times each individual letter (*a, b, c,* and so on) appears in the first 500 letters.

    Enter your results into the Qwerty Questions Frequency Chart: use slashes in the tally column and enter the total number of slashes for each letter into the frequency column.

Use your chart to answer the following questions:

1. What are the two most frequently used letters?

2. Are these the letters you guessed?

3. What are the two letters that were used least?

4. Are these the letters you guessed?

Qwerty Questions Frequency Chart

Letter	Tally	Frequency
a		
b		
c		
d		
e		
f		
g		
h		
i		
j		
k		
l		
m		
n		
o		
p		
q		
r		
s		
t		
u		
v		
w		
x		
y		
z		

Peeking at Presidents

Teacher's Guide

Objective: Students will practice compiling data into chart form; students will construct bar graphs using data from the social studies curriculum.

Prior Knowledge: Students should know how to make a bar graph and how to compile data into chart form.

Time: One or two class periods.

Materials: Activity handouts (3), pencils.

Grouping: Individuals.

New Vocabulary: Bar graph.

Directions:

1. Distribute copies of the activity handouts: Peeking at Presidents and the Presidents Chart (two pages).

2. Review instructions with students. Emphasize that students are to choose *one* category on which to base their study.

3. Give students time to complete their task.

4. Analysis of outcomes (see below).

5. Have students complete their journal entry for this activity.

6. Have volunteers share their journal responses and reactions to other's responses.

Analysis of Outcomes:

The following questions may be used to focus class discussion, reinforce new vocabulary, and extend understandings:

*   What category did you choose?

*   Why did you choose that category?

- Did anything in the Presidents Chart surprise you?

- What other facts would you like to know about these presidents?

Assessment:

- Journal entries

- Evaluating Student Behavior sheets

- Evaluation of responses during discussion

- Evaluation of student bar graphs

* * * * *

The final results of this activity should be posted, or perhaps a booklet could be made. Students might wish to give an oral presentation to the class.

Extension:

The chart can also be used to practice statistical calculations. For example, ask, "What is the average, or mean, number of children in presidents' families?"

As a follow-up activity, have students research and report on other interesting facts about presidents.

See extension for activity 11.

Peeking at Presidents

Using the Presidents Chart, choose *one* category and compile the data for all 39 presidents into chart form. Make a bar graph of your results.

Presidents Chart (part a)

President	Height	Astrological Sign	Birth State	College Attended	Number of Children	Religion
Washington	6'2"+	Pisces	Virginia	None	0	Episcopalian
John Adams	5'6"-5'8"	Scorpio	Massachusetts	Harvard	2	Unitarian
Jefferson	6'2"+	Aries	Virginia	William & Mary	6	no affiliation
Madison	5'4"-5'6"	Pisces	Virginia	Princeton	0	Episcopalian
Monroe	6'0"-6'2"	Taurus	Virginia	William & Mary	3	Episcopalian
John Quincy Adams	5'6"-5'8"	Cancer	Massachusetts	Harvard	4	Unitarian
Jackson	6'0"-6'2"	Pisces	South Carolina	none	0	Presbyterian
Van Buren	5'6"-5'8"	Sagittarius	New York	none	4	Dutch Reformed
William Harrison	5'8"-5'10"	Aquarius	Virginia	Hampden-Sydney	10	Episcopalian
Tyler	6'0"-6'2"	Aries	Virginia	William & Mary	15	Episcopalian
Polk	5'8"-5'10"	Scorpio	North Carolina	North Carolina	0	Presbyterian
Taylor	5'8"-5'10"	Sagittarius	Virginia	none	6	Episcopalian
Fillmore	5'8"-5'10"	Capricorn	New York	none	2	Unitarian
Pierce	5'10"-6'0"	Sagittarius	New Hampshire	Bowdoin	3	Episcopalian
Buchanan	6'0"-6'2"	Taurus	Pennsylvania	Dickinson	0	Presbyterian
Lincoln	6'2"+	Aquarius	Kentucky	none	4	no affiliation
Andrew Johnson	5'10"-6'0"	Capricorn	North Carolina	none	5	no affiliation
Grant	5'8"-5'10"	Taurus	Ohio	West Point	4	Methodist
Hayes	5'8"-5'10"	Libra	Ohio	Kenyon	8	Methodist
Garfield	6'0"-6'2"	Scorpio	Ohio	Williams	7	Disciples of Christ

Presidents Chart (part b)

President	Height	Astrological Sign	Birth State	College Attended	Number of Children	Religion
Arthur	6'0"-6'2"	Libra	Vermont	Union	3	Episcopalian
Cleveland	5'10"-6'0"	Pisces	New Jersey	none	5	Presbyterian
Benjamin Harrison	5'6"-5'8"	Leo	Ohio	Miami (Ohio)	3	Presbyterian
McKinley	5'6"-5'8"	Aquarius	Ohio	Allegheny	2	Methodist
Theodore Roosevelt	5'8"-5'10"	Scorpio	New York	Harvard	6	Dutch Reformed
Taft	6'2"+	Virgo	Ohio	Yale	3	Unitarian
Wilson	5'8"-5'10"	Capricorn	Virginia	Princeton	3	Presbyterian
Harding	6'0"-6'2"	Scorpio	Ohio	Ohio Central	0	Baptist
Coolidge	5'8"-5'10"	Cancer	Vermont	Amherst	2	Congregationalist
Hoover	5'8"-5'10"	Leo	Iowa	Stanford	2	Quaker
Franklin Roosevelt	6'2"+	Aquarius	New York	Harvard	6	Episcopalian
Truman	5'8"-5'10"	Taurus	Missouri	none	1	Baptist
Eisenhower	5'8"-5'10"	Libra	Texas	West Point	2	Presbyterian
Kennedy	6'0"-6'2"	Gemini	Massachusetts	Harvard	3	Catholic
Lyndon Johnson	6'2"+	Virgo	Texas	Southwest Texas State	2	Disciples of Christ
Nixon	5'8"-5'10"	Capricorn	California	Whittier	2	Quaker
Ford	6'0"-6'2"	Cancer	Nebraska	Michigan	4	Episcopalian
Carter	5'8"-5'10"	Libra	Georgia	Annapolis	4	Baptist
Reagan	6'0"-6'2"	Aquarius	Illinois	Eureka	4	Disciples of Christ

Poll Cats

Teacher's Guide

Objective: Students will develop a question, conduct a poll, and present their results in a series of bar graphs as an experience in formulating and solving a problem that involves collecting and analyzing data.

Prior Knowledge: Students should have a strategy for compiling data; students should know how to make a bar graph.

Time: Two or three class periods.

Materials: Activity handouts (2), blank paper, pencils.

Grouping: Individuals.

New Vocabulary: Poll.

Directions:

1. Distribute copies of the activity handouts: Poll Cats and Poll Cats Follow-up Questions.

2. Review instructions with students.

3. Give students time to formulate their questions.

4. Meet with each student to make sure that his or her question is well defined and that it will produce only "yes" or "no" responses. However, the question should not be so general that the student will have trouble charting the responses. An example of a question that might be used is, "What is your favorite sport?"

5. Give students time to complete their task.

6. Have students present their results to the class.

7. Analysis of outcomes (see below).

8. Have students complete their journal entry for this activity.

9. Have volunteers share their journal responses and reactions to other's responses.

Analysis of Outcomes:

The following questions may be used to focus class discussion, reinforce new vocabulary, and extend understandings:

- Did your prediction for the most popular answer accurately reflect the results of your poll?

- Were there differences between girls' answers and boys' answers?

- If so, why do you think this happened?

- Do you think you would have gotten different responses if you had polled teachers instead of students?

- When you look at the results of any poll, how important do you think it is to have information about who was polled?

Assessment:

- Journal entries

- Evaluating Student Behavior sheets

- Evaluation of responses during discussion

- Evaluation of student presentations

- Evaluation of student bar graphs

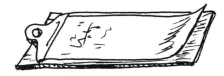

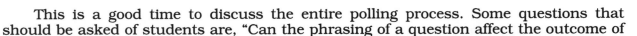

This is a good time to discuss the entire polling process. Some questions that should be asked of students are, "Can the phrasing of a question affect the outcome of the poll?" and, "Can you control the result of a poll by choosing to interview only a certain group of people?"

The bar graphs that students make should be displayed or put into booklet form.

Extension:

Have students investigate and report on current news polls.

Poll Cats

Think of a survey question that you could ask your classmates. For example, "How many hours a night do you watch TV?" or "What is your favorite vegetable?" Write the question in the blank below and have your teacher approve it.

Question:

My prediction of the most popular answer is:

After teacher approval:

1. Poll your classmates, keeping a careful tally of their answers.

2. After you have finished your poll, neatly record the results into a table on a separate piece of paper.

3. Construct three bar graphs of the results—remember to include a title and a scale, and remember to label the horizontal and vertical axes.

   On the first graph, include all answers.

   On the second graph, include just the boys' answers.

   On the third graph, include just the girls' answers.

Poll Cats Follow-up Questions

Answer the following questions about your poll. Use your bar graphs to help you.

1. How many people did you poll?

   a. How many boys?

   b. How many girls?

2. What was the most common response?

3. What was the most common response from girls?

4. What was the most common response from boys?

5. Compare the bar graphs. Did you notice any differences between boys' answers and girls' answers?

6. List the differences you observed:

   a.

   b.

   c.

7. Why do you think there were differences?

8. Did you notice any similarities?

9. List the similarities you observed:

   a.

   b

   c.

10. Why do you think there were similarities?

Dear Parent,

During the coming weeks your child will be using *Chances Are*, a Sense-Able Mathematics investigation of probability and statistics. This program has been specifically designed to correlate with the curriculum and evaluation standards developed by the National Council of Teachers of Mathematics, standards created for strengthening school mathematics programs.

Please take a few minutes to complete and return the attached survey. This will help me understand what your child knows and needs to know. When this unit of study is finished, you will be asked to complete a follow-up survey.

Thank you for encouraging your child to explore the world of mathematics. Your help is greatly appreciated.

Sincerely,

Chances Are
Pre-Program Parent Survey

Student's name:

Your Name:

Date:

Directions: Please complete each of the statements below as honestly as possible without consulting your child. Include comments if you wish.

1. My child feels math is

2. My child becomes confused in math when

3. In the probability and statistics area of mathematics my child already knows

4. This year, in math, I hope my child learns how to

Comments:

Put an *X* on the scale where you think your child belongs. (If you would like, put an *O* on the point where you think *you* belong.)

Math Ability

Not Good   Okay   Good

Chances Are
Pre-Program Self-Assessment

Name: _____

Date: _____

Directions: Complete each of the following statements. There is no right answer. Please answer as honestly as possible. Include comments if you wish.

1. When it's time for math I usually feel _____

    _____

    _____

2. I like math when _____

    _____

    _____

3. I think the hardest part of math is _____

    _____

    _____

4. I get confused in math when _____

    _____

    _____

5. I think the easiest part of math is _____

    _____

    _____

6. I think math is _____

    _____

    _____

7. I get discouraged in math when _____

_____

_____

8. In probability and statistics I already know _____

_____

_____

9. In math I have trouble with _____

_____

_____

10. In probability and statistics I want to know _____

_____

_____

11. The best part of math is _____

_____

_____

12. In math, I hope we _____

_____

_____

Comments:

Put an *X* on the scale where you think you belong.

Math Ability

Not Good   Okay   Good

From *Chances Are.* © 1995. Teacher Ideas Press, P.O. Box 6633, Englewood, CO 80155-6633. 1-800-237-6124.

Evaluating Student Behavior

Student:

Activity:

Learning Behavior Key
    D-Dependent on others
    S-Some support needed
    I-Works independently

Group Behavior Key
    E-Exemplary
    S-Satisfactory
    N-Needs improvement

Learning Behavior	Code	Comments
Comprehends problem (restates and understands the question)		
Develops a plan (applies prior knowledge)		
Applies plan (test hypothesis)		
Organizes and records data		
Modifies plan when necessary		
Persists through to a solution		
Explains plan		
Extends knowledge (relates ideas to other problems)		
Group Behavior	**Code**	**Comments**
Shares		
Cooperates		
Participates		
Initiates		

Observed by:

Date:

From *Chances Are.* © 1995. Teacher Ideas Press, P.O. Box 6633, Englewood, CO 80155-6633. 1-800-237-6124.

Chances Are
Group Assessment

Name: _____

Date: _____

Activity: _____

Assigned Role (if any): _____

Number of Group Members: _____

1. In my group, I helped by _____

_____

_____

2. The best thing about my group was _____

_____

_____

3. We need to improve _____

_____

_____

4. Our group solved the problem by _____

_____

_____

5. The thing that helped us most was _____

_____

_____

6. I learned _____

_____

_____

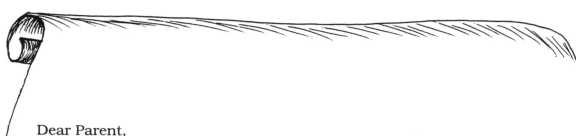

Dear Parent,

Your child has completed a hands-on study of probability and statistics. I would like to know how your child now feels about math in general and probability and statistics in particular.

Please take a few minutes to complete the attached follow-up survey. Once again, your help is greatly appreciated.

Sincerely,

Chances Are
Follow-up Parent Survey

Student's name:

Your Name:

Date:

Directions: Please complete each of the statements below as honestly as possible without consulting your child. Include comments if you wish.

1. My child now feels math is

2. My child becomes confused in probability and statistics when

3. In probability and statistics my child now knows

4. In probability and statistics I would also like my child to learn

Comments:

The ✓ represents your pre-program response. Put an *X* on the scale where you think your child belongs now.

Math Ability

Not Good   Okay   Good

Chances Are
Follow-up Self-Assessment

Name: _____

Date: _____

Directions: Complete each of the following statements. There is no right answer. Please answer as honestly as possible. Include comments if you wish.

1. During *Chances Are* I usually felt _____

   _____

   _____

2. In probability and statistics, I liked when _____

   _____

   _____

3. I think the hardest part of probability and statistics is _____

   _____

   _____

4. I get confused in probability and statistics when _____

   _____

   _____

5. I think the easiest part of probability and statistics is _____

   _____

   _____

6. I think probability and statistics is _____

   _____

   _____

7. I get discouraged in probability and statistics when _____

   _____

   _____

8. In probability and statistics I now know _____

    _____

    _____

9. In probability and statistics I would like to know _____

    _____

    _____

Comments:

The ✓ represents your pre-program response. Put an *X* on the scale where you think you belong now.

Math Ability

Not Good   Okay   Good

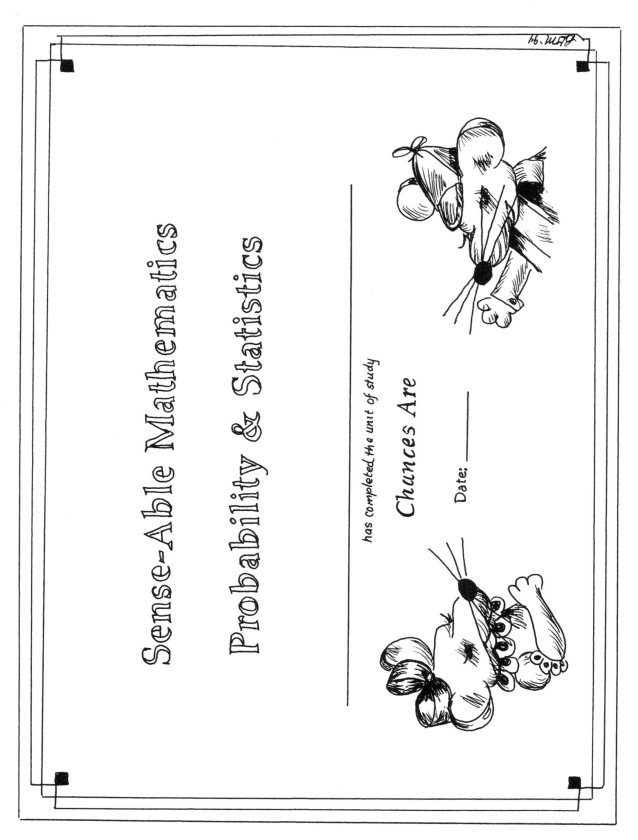

Sense-Able Mathematics

Probability & Statistics

has completed the unit of study

Chances Are

Date: _____

Student Journal

MY JOURNAL FOR

CHANCES ARE

NAME _____

SAM's Crayon Craziness
Journal Entry for Activity 1

Date: _____

I used the colors _____ and _____ .

I found _____ ways to color the boxes.

I liked _____

_____

_____

_____

I learned _____

_____

_____

_____

Comments:

Traffic Stopper
Journal Entry for Activity 2

Date: _____

I used the colors _____ , _____ , and

_____ .

I found _____ ways to design the traffic light.

The difference between this activity and the crayon activity is _____

_____

_____

_____

I liked _____

_____

_____

_____

I learned _____

_____

_____

_____

Comments:

Creative Creatures
Journal Entry for Activity 3

Date: _____

Put a check by the pieces you used:

_____ H1	_____ H2	_____ H3
_____ B1	_____ B2	_____ B3
_____ L1	_____ L2	_____ L3

We created _____ different creatures.

Our strategy was _____

_____

_____

_____

I learned that the number of possible creatures is determined by _____

_____

_____

_____

_____

Comments:

Menu Madness
Journal Entry for Activity 4

Date: _____

Put a check by the place you worked:

_____ SAMburgers
_____ Ben & Cherries
_____ Deli SAMwiches

I made _____

_____

_____

I found _____ different things to put on my menu.

I found these things by _____

_____

_____

The hardest part was _____

_____

_____

The best name I made up was _____

_____

_____

Comments:

It's a Wrap!
Journal Entry for Activity 5

Date: ———————————————————

I know that a *sample space* is defined as ————————————————

—————————————————————————————————————

—————————————————————————————————————

I know that the *probability* of an event is defined as ——————————————

—————————————————————————————————————

—————————————————————————————————————

I thought that the table made the questions ————————————————

—————————————————————————————————————

—————————————————————————————————————

I noticed that ———————————————————————————

—————————————————————————————————————

—————————————————————————————————————

Now I know ————————————————————————————

—————————————————————————————————————

—————————————————————————————————————

I still want to know ——————————————————————————

—————————————————————————————————————

—————————————————————————————————————

Comments:

From *Chances Are.* © 1995. Teacher Ideas Press, P.O. Box 6633, Englewood, CO 80155-6633. 1-800-237-6124.

Dressing up Probability
Journal Entry for Activity 6

Date: _____

The branches in a probability tree show me _____

_____

_____

_____

I predict that if I add green and yellow socks to my wardrobe of two T-shirts and two pairs of shorts, I will have _____ different outfits.

A new strategy I learned is _____

_____

_____

_____

This made me think of _____

_____

_____

_____

Now I can _____

_____

_____

_____

Comments:

Painter's Cap Possibilities
Journal Entry for Activity 7

Date: —————————————————

I think that the best part of this activity was —————————

———————————————————————————

———————————————————————————

———————————————————————————

One thing that still confuses me in probability is ——————

———————————————————————————

———————————————————————————

———————————————————————————

In probability, now I understand ——————————————

———————————————————————————

———————————————————————————

———————————————————————————

A tree diagram helps me ————————————————

———————————————————————————

———————————————————————————

———————————————————————————

Comments:

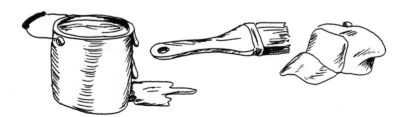

SAM and Samantha's Family Tree
Journal Entry for Activity 8

Date: _____

The probability of a baby being a boy is _____

_____

The family tree diagram I made has _____ branches. This means

_____

_____

_____

The probability of a family like SAM's (three boys and two girls) is _____

_____

_____

I was confused when _____

_____

_____

_____

A good way to improve this activity is _____

_____

_____

Comments:

See How They Run
Journal Entry for Activity 9

Date: —————————————————————

The tree diagram I made for the race has ———————————— branches.

This means that ————————————————————————————————

———

———

———

———

If SAM filled out an entry blank for each possible lineup, he would need ——————————

entry blanks.

The tree helped me ————————————————————————————————

———

———

———

———

I think the best way to show a sample space is to ————————————————————

———

———

———

Comments

Probability Spin-Off
Journal Entry for Activity 10

Date:_____

My experiment showed me that probability is _____

_____

I wonder if _____

_____

_____

_____

This experiement made me realize _____

_____

_____

_____

I know that *empirical* means _____

_____

_____

_____

I know that *theoretical* means _____

_____

_____

_____

Comments:

From *Chances Are.* © 1995. Teacher Ideas Press, P.O. Box 6633, Englewood, CO 80155-6633. 1-800-237-6124.

Qwerty Questions
Journal Entry for Activity 11

Date: _____

If I didn't have the table, I would have tried to organize the data by _____

_____

_____

_____

The table helped me see _____

_____

_____

_____

I predicted that the two most commonly used keys were the letters_____
and _____ .

My data shows the two most commonly used letters are_____ and
_____ .

After comparing my prediction with the data, I discovered _____

_____

_____

_____

After comparing my data with a classmate, I learned that _____

_____

_____

_____

Comments:

Peeking at Presidents
Journal Entry for Activity 12

Date: _____

The most interesting thing I found in the chart of presidents is _____

_____

_____

I was surprised to see that_____

_____

_____

The topic I chose was _____

_____

_____

I chose this topic because _____

_____

_____

I had trouble with_____

_____

_____

The thing I would like to know about the presidents that is not in the chart, is_____

_____

_____

To find the answer to this question I should _____

_____

_____

Poll Cats
Journal Entry for Activity 13

Date: _____

The question I asked was _____

_____

Taking this poll showed me _____

_____

The hardest thing about making the bar graphs was _____

_____

The thing I liked most about this project was _____

_____

After looking at other students' graphs respond to the following:

I was most surprised by the answers to the question about_____

_____

I was surprised because _____

_____

I was least surprised by the answers to the question about_____

_____

I wasn't surprised by the answers because _____

_____

The question on which most boys and girls agreed *with each other* is about _____

_____

The question on which most boys and girls disagreed is _____

_____

Comments:

* * * * *

I have finished *Chances Are!* Now I realize that _____

_____

Curriculum and Evaluation Standards
for School Mathematics

In grades K-4, the mathematics curriculum should include experiences with data analysis and probability so that students can

- collect, organize, and describe data;

- construct, read, and interpret displays of data;

- formulate and solve problems that involve collecting and analyzing data;

- explore concepts of chance.

In grades 5-8, the mathematics curriculum should include explorations of probability in real-world situations so that students can

- model situations by devising and carrying out experiments of simulations to determine probabilities;

- model situations by constructing a sample space to determine probabilities;

- appreciate the power of using a probability model by comparing experimental results with mathematical expectations;

- make predictions that are based on experimental or theoretical probabilities;

- develop an appreciation for the pervasive use of probability in the real world.

Making Manipulatives

Let your creative side take over when creating three-dimensional manipulatives. The following are only suggestions to get you started. You and your students might have better ideas on how to construct these and other items. Take a look around your classroom for materials. Have fun and enjoy your creations.

Plastic notebook binders (as many colors as possible). Shapes can be cut to represent ham slices, cheese (don't forget the holes for Swiss), tomatoes, onion, lettuce, and so on.

Oaktag (red, green, white, yellow). If binders are unavailable, substitute oaktag. Laminate the oaktag shapes to increase their life expectancy.

Sponges (1/8-inch to 1/2-inch thick, white to light-yellow). Sponges can be used to create slices of bread and hamburger rolls. Cut the sponge into the desired shape and color the edge (the "crust") with a brown marker to achieve a more realistic appearance; use a black marker to add dots (seeds). Sponges can also be used to create ice cream cones. Cut the sponge into the desired shape and use a marker to put on a crosshatch pattern.

Scouring pads (not steel-wool). The pad can be used to create hamburger patties. Cut to shape and color brown or black with markers.

algorithm. A rule, formula, or method for solving a particular type of problem.

bar graph. A graph in which the length or height of each bar is scaled to represent a number of data items.

empirical results. The actual outcomes obtained by performing an experiment. Students might wish to conduct their own probability experiments and tabulate the results. It should be pointed out that these results can vary widely. Just because the theoretical probability of a tossed coin landing heads is 1/2 does not mean that if a student tosses a coin twice it will come up heads one time and tails the other. Nor does it mean that if a student tosses a coin 1,000 times it will be heads exactly 500 times and tails exactly 500 times. *On each toss* the probability of heads is 1/2. What students should know about empirical data is that if the experiment is fair, the more times it is repeated the closer their empirical results should be to the theoretical predictions. (For example, they might toss the coin 1,000 times and get 490 tails and 510 heads, which is fairly close to predictions based on the probability of 1/2 for each outcome.)

event. An outcome or a series of possible outcomes in an experiment. For example, in an experiment consisting of rolling a die, an event might be rolling the number 2, rolling an even number, or rolling a number with a name that starts with the letter *t*.

experiment. Usually refers to an action or a set of actions to be performed. Examples: tossing a coin; rolling a die; drawing a name from a box of names; drawing three cards from a deck.

outcome. One possible result of an experiment. Examples: a coin landing heads up; a die showing the number 4; drawing the name "John" from a box of names; drawing the four of hearts, the two of spades, and the ace of spades.

permutation and combination. The term *permutation* is merely an arrangement of a given number of objects. The term *combination* is used in probability when the order of an arrangement is not important. For example: Suppose that the Scrabble® tiles with the letters *A*, *B*, and *C* are face down in a box. If two tiles are chosen, there are three possible combination: *A* and *B*, *A* and *C*, or *B* and *C*. No matter which letter is chosen first, there can be only three combinations. However, if the two tiles are used to fill in two spaces on the Scrabble® board, the arrangement *AB* is different than the arrangement *BA*. With three tiles there are six permutations (arrangements): *AB, BA, AC, CA, BC,* and *CB*.

Perhaps a more easily understood example would be: Suppose there are five students—Tom, Dick, Harry, Sue, and Linda. Each student's name is written on a separate piece of paper. The papers are folded and put into a bag. Three names are drawn, one at a time, from the bag. The student whose name is drawn first will receive $50, the student whose name is drawn second will receive $20, and the third student will receive $10. The order in which the names are drawn is important. Drawing Sue, Dick, Tom is different than drawing Dick, Sue, Tom. In this experiment, we would be interested in the number of permutations of the names. In fact, there is a sample space of 60 permutations (5 choices for the first draw x 4 remaining choices for the second draw x 3 remaining choices for the third draw = 60). If, however, this method is used to form a committee of three people, the order in which the names are drawn no longer matters. A committee of Tom, Dick, and Sue is exactly the same as a committee of Sue, Tom, and Dick. In this experiment, we would be concerned with the number of combinations of names. In either case there are 60 permutations, but only 10 combinations.

Though such experiments are beyond the scope of the intermediate grade-level curriculum, the *distinction* between combination and permutation is understandable here. It will be helpful to students later if the teacher is careful to use the correct terms now.

poll. A poll is a survey of a selected group of individuals that compiles their responses to a specific question or questions.

probability of an event. The probability of an event is a number between 0 and 1, inclusive. Impossible events have a probability of 0 (the probability of rolling an eight with a standard six-sided die). An event that is a "sure thing" has a probability of 1 (the probability of rolling a number less than eight with a standard six-sided die). The probability of an event is defined as the number of successful outcomes divided by the total number of outcomes. For example, in rolling a standard six-sided die there are six possible outcomes: 1, 2, 3, 4, 5, and 6. Two of these outcomes are numbers that begin with the letter *t* when spelled out—*two* and *three*. It follows that the probability of rolling a number whose name starts with the letter *t* would be 2/6 (or 1/3 if you reduce the fraction). In mathematical symbols this is written:

P(number that begins with the letter *t*) = 2/6

sample space. The set of *all* possible outcomes of an experiment. Examples: the sample space for tossing a coin would be {heads, tails}; the sample space for rolling a standard six-sided die would be {1, 2, 3, 4, 5, 6}. (It is standard mathematical notation to enclose the set of outcomes in brackets.)

statistics. The branch of mathematics that involves the collection, organization, and interpretation of numerical data.

theoretical prediction. First, find the probability of an event using the formula given under the definition of probability of an event. This formula assumes a "fair" experiment, one in which each of the possible outcomes has an equally likely chance of occurring. Now, a theoretical prediction for that event can be calculated by multiplying the probability of the event by the number of like actions in the experiment. For example, in an experiment consisting of tossing a coin 20 times, where the probability of an outcome of tails is 1/2, it is theoretically predicted (i.e., calculated) that there will be 10 (1/2 x 20 = 10) outcomes that are tails.

tree diagram. A diagram used to show the total number of possible outcomes for a probability experiment. For example, in an experiment in which a coin will be tossed three times, the tree diagram below shows all possible outcomes:

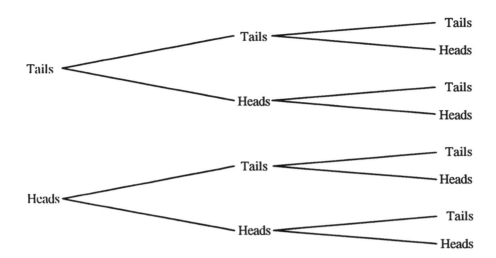

Notice that the number of possible outcomes of an experiment can be found by counting the number of rightmost outer branches of the tree, in this case.

Anderson, L. M. 1981. *Student responses to seatwork: Implications for the study of student's cognitive processing.* Research Series, no. 102. East Lansing: Institute for Research on Teaching, Michigan State University.

Brophy, J., and T. Good. 1986. Teacher behavior and student achievement. In *Research on teaching handbook,* 3d ed., edited by M. C. Wittrock. New York: Macmillan.

Bruner, Jerome S. 1960. *The process of education.* Cambridge: Harvard University Press.

Carpenter, T. P., J. Hiebert, and J. M. Moses. 1983. The effect of instruction on children's solution of addition and subtraction problems. In *Educational studies in mathematics.* Dordrecht, Holland; Boston: D. Reidel.

Doyle, W. 1983. Academic work. *Review of Educational Research,* 53: 159-200.

Kirby, J. R., ed. 1984. *Cognitive strategies and educational performance.* Orlando, FL: Academic Press.

National Council of Teachers of Mathematics (NCTM). 1987. *Curriculum and evaluation standards for school mathematics.* Working draft. Reston, VA: NCTM.

National Council of Teachers of Mathematics (NCTM). 1989. *New directions for elementary school mathematics.* Reston, VA: NCTM.

Peterson, P. L. 1979. Direct instruction reconsider. In *Research on teaching: Concepts, finding and implications,* edited by P. L. Peterson and H. J. Walberg. Berkeley, CA: McCutchan.

Peterson, P. L., and T. C. Janicki. 1979. Individual characteristics and children's learning in large-group and small-group approaches. *Journal of Educational Research* 22, no. 3: 309-35.

Peterson, P. L., T. C. Janicki, and S. R. Swing. 1981. Ability X treatment interaction effects on children's learning in large-group and small-group approaches. *American Education Research Journal,* 18: 453-73.

Peterson, P. L., L. C. Wilkinson, F. Spinelli, and S. R. Swing. 1984. Merging the process-product and the sociolinguistic paradigm. In *The social context of instruction: Group organization and group processes.* Orlando, FL: Academic Press.

Pressley, M., and J. R. Levin, eds. 1983a. *Cognitive strategy research: Educational applications.* New York: Springer-Verlag.

Pressley, M., and J. R. Levin, eds. 1983b. *Cognitive strategy research: Psychological foundation.* New York: Springer-Verlag.

Rosenshine, B. V. 1979. Content, time, and direct instruction. In *Research on teaching: Concepts, finding and implications,* edited by P. L. Peterson and H. J. Walberg. Berkeley, CA: McCutchan.

Rosenshine, B., and R. Stevens. 1984. Classroom instruction in reading. In *Handbook of reading research*, edited by P. D. Pearson. New York: Longman.

Weinstein, C. F., and R. F. Mayer. 1986. The teaching of learning strategies. In *Research on teaching handbook*, 3d ed., edited by M. C. Wittrock. New York: Macmillan.

About the Authors

Sheila Dolgowich is a former computer programmer/systems analyst. She has taught mathematics from kindergarten through the graduate level and currently is the District Computer Coordinator in a centralized school. Sheila holds a bachelor of science degree in mathematics from the State University of New York at Oneonta and master of science degrees in mathematics and mathematics education from the State University of New York at Albany.

Helen Lounsbury is a career teacher with more than 30 years of experience at primary, intermediate, middle school, high school, and graduate levels. Helen holds a bachelor of science degree from the State University of New York at New Paltz and a master of art degree in children's literature and curriculum development from Norwich University.

Barry Muldoon is an art teacher at an elementary school in upstate New York. He has worked as a commercial artist and as an art educator in grades K-12. Barry holds an associate degree in advertising, art, and design from the State University of New York at Farmingdale, a bachelor of science degree in art education, and a master of art degree from Hofstra University.

The authors are experienced in K-12 curriculum development. They are frequent presenters and participants at education conferences throughout the country.